To my FRI[...]
AARON + DONNIE

May God Bless your
Reading

Byron Allen, Jr.

THE PRAYING PROPHET

THE PRAYING PROPHET

A CONVERSATION WITH GOD
ABOUT PRAYER
STUDIES IN HABAKKUK

REVISED EDITION

Dr. Byron Allen, Jr.

XULON PRESS

Xulon Press
2301 Lucien Way #415
Maitland, FL 32751
407.339.4217
www.xulonpress.com

This is a revision of the first edition, which was published in 2019 under the title HABAKKUK. The corrections and additions included here will both enlarge and enhance the content as well as make reading it easier.

Unless otherwise indicated, Scripture quotations taken from the King James Version (KJV)–*public domain.*

Paperback ISBN-13: 978-1-6628-0930-9

eBook ISBN-13: 978-1-6628-0931-6

Table of Contents

The Praying Prophet

A CONVERSATION WITH GOD
ABOUT PRAYER
a fresh and unique approach to the book of Habakkuk

T his is a study of the Bible book of Habakkuk as a book about *prayer*. The thoughts contained in this study of Habakkuk are the results of my meditations on the Word of God collected from my files of more than sixty years as pastor of Baptist churches. They are not put forward as a final, authoritative interpretation. The Scriptures speak to, and minister to, the heart of individuals in various ways, which are somewhat dependent upon the circumstances in which God places each person. This study contains a fresh and unique approach to the contents of the Book of Habakkuk.

It will be observed, as you read these studies, that I favor a more literal translation and interpretation of the Scriptures like that of the King James Version. It will be noted that I have included in parentheses the words of the earlier versions of the Bible, basically the Hebrew and Greek versions. The reader who is unfamiliar with these languages can ignore these parentheses without adversely affecting the understanding of the thought of the language or the thought being presented in these studies.

May God bless those who read these devotional thoughts.

Your friend in the Lord Jesus Christ:
Dr. Byron Allen, Jr.

As this study progresses, I will insert a series of PRECEPTS. These will emphasize the general truth, or the theme of, the following section of the study of Habakkuk.

"THE BURDEN OF HABAKKUK"

Chapter One

The Praying Prophet

A CONVERSATION WITH GOD ABOUT PRAYER
a fresh and unique approach to the study of Habakkuk

The burden which Habakkuk the prophet did see.

A conversation took place about 2,600 years ago. The subject of that conversation was prayer—more specifically unanswered prayer. The conversation took place because one person thought a prayer was not answered. It may seem an impossibility, but that conversation was recorded. One of the principal characters involved in the conversation made a record of what was discussed. The conversation was not a privileged conversation; therefore, no trust was violated in making the copy. In fact, one person involved in the conversation suggested that the offended party make a copy. The party was even told to make the copy clear and plain to enable future generations to read it in a hurry and still understand the plainly written message.

Now, you may be asking: "How do you know so much about such an ancient conversation? If it took place 2,600 years ago, how could any person in today's world know so much about it?" My initial response is that a copy was made of the conversation that has survived the intervening years of history and is available for any person to read. In fact, I have read and studied that copy. Let me tell you just how that came about.

I stretched out on my bed one evening intending to lie there and read for a while. I had formed a habit over the years of reading for a period of time each night before turning out the light and going to sleep. I was rather casually reading the Bible book of Habakkuk in the Old Testament. This particular evening was unexpectedly different from what others had been. My mind was just blown away as I realized that I was reading the record of a conversation that occurred 2,600 years ago. I was reading a record of a conversation between God and Habakkuk. The record of that conversation is actually the Bible book of Habakkuk.

The record of the conversation has been available to us for all the centuries. It has been read, discussed, taught, and considered as a statement of prophecy. But that evening I discovered that the subject of that conversation was prayer. Habakkuk had prayed, and it seemed to him that God had not heard or answered. He then made a record of his discussion with God about not answering his prayer.

PRECEPT # 1
To become God's messenger is to carry a burden

There is essentially nothing known about Habakkuk the person. The first verse of the book gives some very brief and basic information. The verse reads:

The burden which Habakkuk the prophet did see.

The verse provides information for the title of this book. It also gives the name of the author. Little is known about Habakkuk the prophet. The verse simply gives his name and designates him as a prophet. The name Habakkuk (khab·ak·kook-חֲבַקּוּק) is usually traced to the Hebrew verb khaw·bak (חָבַק), which means "to fold one's hands" or "to embrace." There is some debate as to whether the verb is in the active or the passive voice. Does it mean that Habakkuk did the "embracing"? Or does it mean that Habakkuk was the one "embraced"?

It is possible that the complaint recorded in 1:2 is based upon Habakkuk's burden for the people of the nation of Judah.

O LORD, how long shall I cry, and thou wilt not hear! even cry out unto thee of violence, and thou wilt not save!

Implied in this verse is the possibility that he has become so burdened for Judah that he felt constrained to offer intense prayer for God's intervention and salvation of his people. He was so burdened for the salvation of Judah that he believed God was the only hope of the nation. This would explain his complaint in which he charged God with a non-answer to his prayer.

Some who write of their studies concerning this matter see Habakkuk's name suggesting that he is one who embraced his people to comfort and uphold them. Others, however, see Habakkuk as one who embraced the problem of divine justice in a wicked world. It is true; he did that very well. It is also possible that the name tells us that Habakkuk is one who embraced God. Still others prefer the passive voice—in which his name is used—and picture Habakkuk as one embraced by God as His child and messenger. All of these ideas may give some significant insight into the meaning of the name Habakkuk.

The name Habakkuk appears only twice in the Hebrew Bible. It is used in Habakkuk 1:1 and again in Habakkuk 3:1. There is no biographical information available about him. Nothing is known about his parents, his hometown, his education, or his occupation. Our knowledge of the person named Habakkuk is limited to his being designated a prophet. It was as a prophet that he had a conversation with God. Each of these two verses in which Habakkuk's name appears have characteristics which give us some significant information about the prophet.

Chapter 1, verse 1 reads:

The burden which Habakkuk the prophet did see.

First, notice the definite article *the* is used in 1:1, making the burden specific. The focus is on one and only one *burden*. Habakkuk *did see* this specific burden. By using the particular word for *see* Habakkuk is telling us that he not only saw the burden physically, but he also saw it with his intelligence. The prophets were known as *seers* because God frequently communicated his message to them through the medium of *visions*. Habakkuk is therefore claiming to have received such a *vision* from God. He is also indicating that he understood the content and meaning of the *vision*. The book he authored is his account of the existential process by which he arrived at his understanding of the *vision*.

Chapter 3, verse 1 reads:

A prayer of Habakkuk the prophet upon Shigionoth.

Notice here the use of the indefinite article *a*. By using this article, the writer places the focus on a generic prayer. He does not so much call attention to a specific prayer but rather gives an example of the general characteristics of Habakkuk's prayer life after he has come to *see* (understand) how God communicates with him in answering his prayers. Jesus gave us a *Model Prayer* which is commonly known as *The Lord's Prayer*. But it is actually only a *model*. The prayer of Habakkuk recorded in chapter 3 is, in similar fashion, *A Model Prayer*.

The following is a copy of the book of Habakkuk, showing the possible flow of that conversation:

INTRODUCTION: (1:1)

The burden which Habakkuk the prophet did see.

HABAKKUK: (1:2-4).

O LORD, how long shall I cry, and you will not hear! even cry out unto you of violence, and you will not save! Why do you show me iniquity and cause me to behold grievance? for spoiling and violence are before me: and there are that raise up strife and contention. Therefore, the law is slacked, and judgment does never go forth: for the wicked do compass about the righteous; therefore, wrong judgment proceeds.

GOD: (1:5-11)

Behold you among the heathen, and regard, and wonder marvelously: for I will work a work in your days, which you will not believe, though it be told you. For, lo, I raise up the Chaldeans, that bitter and hasty nation, which shall march through the breadth of the land, to possess the dwelling places that are not theirs. They are terrible and dreadful: their judgment and their dignity shall proceed of themselves. Their horses also are swifter than the leopards and are more fierce than the evening wolves: and their horsemen shall spread themselves, and their horsemen shall come from far; they shall fly as the eagle that hastens to eat. They shall come all for violence: their faces shall sup up as the east wind, and they shall gather the captivity as the sand. And they shall scoff at the kings, and the princes shall be a scorn unto them: they shall deride every strong hold; for they shall heap dust and take it. Then shall his mind change, and he shall pass over, and offend, imputing this his power unto his god.

HABAKKUK: (1:12-17)

Are you not from everlasting, O LORD my God, my Holy One? we shall not die. O LORD, you have ordained them for judgment; and, O mighty God, you have established them for correction. You are of purer eyes than to behold evil, and cannot look on iniquity: wherefore look you upon them that deal treacherously, and hold your tongue when the wicked devours the man that is more righteous than he? And make men as the fishes of the sea, as the creeping things, that have no ruler over them? They take up all of them with the angle, they catch them in their net, and gather them in their drag: therefore, they rejoice and are glad. Therefore, they sacrifice unto their net, and burn incense unto their drag; because by them their portion is fat, and their meat plenteous. Shall they therefore empty their net, and not spare continually to slay the nations?

HABAKKUK: (2:1)

I will stand upon my watch, and set me upon the tower, and will watch to see what he will say unto me, and what I shall answer when I am reproved.

GOD: (2:2-20)

And the LORD answered me, and said, Write the vision, and make it plain upon tables, that he may run that reads it. For the vision is yet for an appointed time, but at the end it shall speak, and not lie: though it tarry, wait for it; because it will surely come, it will not tarry. Behold, his soul which is lifted up is not upright in him: but the just shall live by his faith.

Yes also, because he transgresses by wine, he is a proud man, neither keeps at home, who enlarges his desire as hell, and is as death, and cannot be satisfied, but gathers unto him all nations, and heaps unto him all people: Shall not all these take up a parable against him, and a taunting proverb against him, and say, Woe to him that increases that which is not his! how long? and to him that loads himself with thick clay! Shall they not rise up suddenly that shall bite you, and awake that shall vex you, and you shall be for booties unto them? Because you have spoiled many nations, all the remnant of the people shall spoil you; because of men's blood, and for the violence of the land, of the city, and of all that dwell therein. Woe to him that covets an evil covetousness to his house, that he may set his nest on high, that he may be delivered from the power of evil! You have consulted shame to your house by cutting off many people and have sinned against your soul. For the stone shall cry out of the wall, and the beam out of the timber shall answer it. Woe to him that builds a town with blood and establishes a city by iniquity! Behold, is it not of the LORD of hosts that the people shall labor in the very fire, and the people shall weary them-selves for very vanity? For the earth shall be filled with the knowledge of the glory of the LORD, as the waters cover the sea.

Woe unto him that gives his neighbor drink, that puts your bottle to him, and make him drunk also, that you may look on their nakedness! You are filled with shame for glory: drink you also, and let your uncircumcision be revealed: the cup of the LORD'S right hand shall be turned unto you, and shameful spewing shall be on your glory. For the violence of Lebanon shall cover you, and the spoil of beasts, which made them afraid, because of men's blood, and for the violence of the land, of the city, and of all that dwell therein. What profits the graven image that the maker thereof has graven it; the molten image, and a teacher of lies, that the maker of his work trusts therein, to make dumb idols? Woe unto him that says to the wood, Awake; to the dumb stone, Arise, it shall teach! Behold, it is laid over with gold and silver, and there is no breath at all in the midst of it. But the LORD is in his holy temple: let all the earth keep silence before him.

HABAKKUK'S PRAYER: (3:1-19)

A prayer of Habakkuk the prophet upon Shigionoth.

O LORD, I have heard your speech, and was afraid: O LORD, revive your work in the midst of the years, in the midst of the years make known; in wrath remember mercy.

God came from Teman, and the Holy One from mount Paran. Selah. His glory covered the heavens, and the earth was full of his praise. And his brightness was as the light; he had horns coming out of his hand: and there was the hiding of his power. Before him went the pestilence, and burning coals went forth at his feet. He stood, and measured the earth: he beheld, and drove asunder the nations; and the everlasting mountains were scattered, the perpetual hills did bow: his ways are everlasting. I saw the tents of Cushan in affliction: and the curtains of the land of Midian did tremble. Was the

*LORD displeased against the rivers? was your
anger against the rivers? was your wrath against
the sea, that you did ride upon your horses and
your chariots of salvation? Your bow was made
quite naked, according to the oaths of the tribes,
even your word. Selah. You did cleave the earth
with rivers. The mountains saw you, and they trembled: the overflowing of the water passed by: the
deep uttered his voice and lifted up his hands on
high. The sun and moon stood still in their habitation: at the light of your arrows they went, and at
the shining of your glittering spear. You did march
through the land in indignation, you did thresh
the heathen in anger. You went forth for the salvation of your people, even for salvation with your
anointed; you wounded the head out of the house of
the wicked, by discovering the foundation unto the
neck. Selah. You did strike through with his staves
the head of his villages: they came out as a whirlwind to scatter me: their rejoicing was as to devour
the poor secretly. You did walk through the sea
with your horses, through the heap of great waters.
When I heard, my belly trembled; my lips quivered
at the voice: rottenness entered into my bones, and
I trembled in myself, that I might rest in the day
of trouble: when he comes up unto the people, he
will invade them with his troops. Although the fig
tree shall not blossom, neither shall fruit be in the
vines; the labor of the olive shall fail, and the fields
shall yield no meat; the flock shall be cut off from
the fold, and there shall be no herd in the stalls: Yet
I will rejoice in the LORD, I will joy in the God of*

my salvation. The LORD God is my strength, and
he will make my feet like hinds' feet, and he will
make me to walk upon my high places. To the chief
singer on my stringed instruments.

The first words from Habakkuk form the brief but basic introduction to this very short book. They give a full-color portrait of
Habakkuk's heart and mind and a brief but accurate description of
the book he wrote. Habakkuk is classified as a book of prophecy.
He is labeled as a "minor prophet." However, this study looks at
the book for its lessons about *prayer*. The prophetic element of
Habakkuk is very brief. It is contained in Habakkuk 1:6-11. Those
brief verses are given a minimum amount of space and discussion
in this study because in this study Habakkuk is treated as a book
about prayer in contrast to being a book of prophecy.

Because this book of the Old Testament and its author are classified by the scholars as *minor* and because Habakkuk is seen by
them as a book of *prophecy*, it is often ignored and its lessons
about prayer are overlooked. The truths about prayer taught in
Habakkuk ought to be elevated to a place of more importance
and significance. These facts, plus the character of the prophet
Habakkuk himself, demand that he be seen as a *major* player in
the drama of prayer as it is played out on the stage of Judah and
Babylon. Habakkuk should be seen by his readers as a *major*
pray-er instead of being only classified as a *minor prophet*.

The prophetic element in Habakkuk is not to be discounted.
However, that subject causes many to lose sight of the lessons
about prayer that are clearly seen in the conversation recorded
in the book. The subject of that conversation is *God's response*
to Habakkuk's prayer. The Bible contains the records of many

experiences that persons have had with God in prayer. Abraham interceded for Sodom. Moses prayed for Israel after the gold calf event. Daniel fasted and prayed after reading what Jeremiah wrote about the coming captivity of Judah. Nehemiah prayed and fasted for three months after one of his "brothers" informed him of the deplorable physical and spiritual conditions of Jerusalem. Jesus prayed in the garden. Jesus prayed for his disciples. Paul prayed for the churches he started. But the prayer of Habakkuk is perhaps the most unique and informative of all. Historically, Habakkuk has not been considered as a *praying prophet, though he* really was. The book of Habakkuk is all about his prayer relationship with God.

Prophecy generally has to do with future events; Habakkuk contains a revelation of future events. The events seem to be very imminent. They reveal some basic principles about the ways in which God deals with his people in their sinfulness. In that arena, they reveal something about how God has acted, now acts, and will in the future act, toward sin in our age. But in addition to being a revelation of future events, it is an invaluable source of information about the contemporary prayer experiences of Believers. Habakkuk was a *praying prophet.* Prayer is always a contemporary experience. Modern-day people who pray are generally praying about contemporary circumstances which are relevant for the day.

The book of Habakkuk contains the prophet's complaint. It also records his perception that his prayers were not being heard and answered by God. And the book closes with Habakkuk's prayer song of confession and praise to God, whom Habakkuk is now convinced has been altogether faithful in listening to and answering his prayers. The importance of Habakkuk's transformation is the theme of this study. We can learn from his conversation with God to have assurance in prayer. We are taught through the conversation so very much about God's character and conduct in responding to the prayers of his children.

The operative words in the first verse of Habakkuk are *burden* and *see*. These words appear to be both deliberately and wisely chosen. What did Habakkuk see? What was the nature of the burden? Why did Habakkuk consider that factor a burden? He called it a "burden." The word *masa* (משא), means "a burden" and is used in Proverbs 30:1 and 31:1, where it is translated as *prophecy*. The word *burden* leads one to understand the message that was laid upon the mind of the prophet, and by him pressed on to the attention of the people, was a "weighty" message. The message of the Lord ought not to have been regarded as a burden by the people; but it could not fail to be realized as such by the prophet. It is apparent that Habakkuk at times felt the weight of the message to be a very heavy load. The general public appeared to disbelieve the message. There was a general nationwide failure to respond affirmatively to the message. The majority of the general citizenry questioned the authenticity of the message. They would not accept the fact that it was of divine origin.

Jeremiah 23:33-38 says:

> *And when this people, or the prophet, or a priest, shall ask you, saying, What is the burden of the LORD? you shall then say unto them, What burden? I will even forsake you, says the LORD. And as for the prophet, and the priest, and the people, that shall say, The burden of the LORD, I will even punish that man and his house. You*

*shall say everyone to his neighbor, and everyone
to his brother, What has the LORD answered? and,
What has the LORD spoken? And the burden of
the LORD shall you mention no more: for every
man's word shall be his burden; for you have perverted the words of the living God, of the LORD of
hosts our God. You shall say to the prophet, What
has the LORD answered you? and, What has the
LORD spoken? But since you say, The burden of
the LORD; therefore, the LORD says; Because you
say this word, 'The burden of the LORD, and I
have sent unto you, saying, You shall not say, The
burden of the LORD.*

Any and each pastor of a local church, along with many other religious leaders, whose primary vocation is to facilitate the commu-
nication of God's Word to individuals or to a nation, should feel a
similar "burden" when attempting to aid others in understanding
and applying that word to contemporary society.

The twenty-first century is very young, and its future looks very
challenging. One would have difficulty keeping count of the
wars currently being fought, and there is hardly any way to keep
count of the loss of human life. It appears as if all value attached
to human life has vanished. Witness the continuing discussion
and debate about abortion. The values once attached to society's
structures and institutions are being challenged or even totally
disregarded. Terrorism is a cause for fear to most of the inhabitants of the world. Nature seems to have released all its fury upon
planet earth. Earthquakes, volcanoes, floods, hurricanes, typhoons,
tornadoes, drought, and wildfires rage out of control. And other
such tragedies mount up too rapidly to track. Disease, famine, and

hunger hang like a dark cloud over a large portion of the earth's population. It is little wonder that thinking people are beginning to ask questions. Why is there so much oppression? Why all the injustice? Why do evil men prosper? Why do the righteous suffer? Why doesn't God do something? Why doesn't God clean up this mess? Why? Why? Why?

The content of the book of Habakkuk is, by most Old Testament students, considered a prophecy. Whatever the meaning of his name, Habakkuk was a prophet. More than that, he was a praying prophet. Prophets were praying men; Habakkuk was. Prophets sometimes prayed for those against whom they prophesied. Prophets who were intimately acquainted with the mind of God concerning future events knew how to order their prayers. They knew what to pray for. They prayed with foresight in troublous times. Habakkuk had apparently received God's answer to previous prayers. Therefore, he expected God to be ready to answer his requests, so he repeated his petitions to him. This is what gave birth to the complaint that is the trigger of the conversation that is recorded in this Bible book that bears the name Habakkuk.

The second verse of the book reads as follows:

> *O LORD, how long shall I cry, and thou wilt not hear! even cry out unto thee of violence, and thou wilt not save?*

This verse sets the stage for Habakkuk's encounter with God in the school of prayer.

God's people, those who trust in the one true God who made heaven and earth and who in His sovereignty administers their every movement, and those who look to Him for some response, have taken the Bible as their guide for living, are a people of prayer—sincere, earnest prayer—modeled after those great men and women of the Bible. But sometimes it seems that God is not responding to these pleas.

The record of the conversation has been available to us for all the centuries. It has been read, discussed, taught, and considered as a statement of prophecy. But I discovered that evening that the subject of that conversation was prayer. Habakkuk had prayed, and it seemed to him as though God had not answered. He then made a record of his discussion with God about not answering prayer.

PRECEPT # 2
To become God's messenger is to learn about prayer.

Several years ago I became aware of a form of prayer that the author called Conversational Prayer. That pattern of praying became an indescribable blessing in the church of which I was the pastor. It actually had its greatest appeal among the youth group. I discovered recently (early in 2020) that those who were part of that youth group still remember those days when we used that form of prayer known as Conversational Prayer. My follow-up study of prayer led to the discovery that the prayers of God's people could, for the most part, be placed in one of two categories. They could be classed as either *fellowship oriented* or classified as *circumstance oriented*. This discovery came about as I was reading and meditating on Colossians 4:2 and 1 Thessalonians 5:17.

The verse in Colossians reads:

Continue in prayer and watch in the same with thanksgiving.

The 1 Thessalonians verse says:

Pray without ceasing.

In the Colossians verse the word *continue* means to follow a consistent and regular pattern or to be steadfast. It means to be strong and unremitting in prayer. The words *without ceasing* in the 1 Thessalonians verse means to pray frequently and spontaneously. As I studied the two verses, I came to realize that praying becomes for the most part either *circumstance oriented* or it becomes *fellowship oriented.*

Circumstance oriented prayer means that a Believer is drawn to pray when some issue arises that an individual does not think can be handled alone. This is usually some crisis or issue that is considered to be of such importance or magnitude that it is thought to demand immediate action. The use of *oriented* places the focus of the prayer. The focus is usually directed to the issue for which prayer is demanded and not upon God, to whom the prayer should be directed. The word also draws attention to the motive for the prayer. The circumstances out of which the prayer is birthed give it direction and provide the controlling factors that determine its effectiveness.

On the other hand, *fellowship oriented* prayer means the Believer prays frequently and spontaneously. The Believer also is seen to have a regular and unremitting pattern of fellowship with Jesus Christ.

Circumstance oriented prayer will take the form of a monologue. The believer will be the principal, if not the only, speaker.
Fellowship oriented prayer will take the form of a dialogue, and
both God and the believer will participate in the conversation.

In *circumstance oriented* prayer, a Believer is occupied with telling
God about the felt need and does not listen to hear what God might
say, and therefore prayer becomes a monologue. When one prays
in such a pattern, God is given little opportunity to speak.

In *fellowship oriented* prayer, God and the Believer talk with each
other and the prayer time becomes a dialogue (a conversation).
When this happens, that which would otherwise seem to be a crisis
event becomes a more nearly normal issue in the daily fellowship
between the Lord Jesus and the Believer.

A further illustration of this approach to prayer is found in Psalm
107. The writer of Psalm 107 cites four examples of God delivering of His people. In each of the four examples, the people had
arrived at the conclusion that they were in a situation of need that
left them unable to escape. The only solution was to discover
and bring into the situation someone with plans for their deliverance who possessed power, resources, and wisdom to execute
those plans and bring them to full fruition. In each case the people
pleaded for the Lord to help them out of their distress. And God
helped them as described in verses 6, 13, 19, and 28.

The four sections of the Psalm are probably not intended to be
an inclusive spiritual biography of a person or people. They do,
however, in a representative way, involve all the basic emotions,
endangerments, endearments, estrangements, escapements, and
endeavors of Believers on their journey through an unfriendly

earthly environment. Throughout the Bible the trail followed by the persons and/or people described in this Psalm is illuminated.

The first example was those who took a pathway that led them through some indescribable wilderness where "they wandered in the wilderness in a solitary way." The word *wandered* means "to move about without a fixed course, aim, or goal, or to go astray morally." The word is used to describe someone who staggers as they walk. The word *solitary*, as used here, probably refers to a place of solitude more than to a mood of solitude. They were alone because they were away from God.

In the second paragraph of the Psalm, the people are characterized as "being bound in affliction and iron." The word *affliction* speaks of economic poverty and/or personal, psychological misery. The word *iron* is almost exclusively translated as "iron." It figuratively refers to harshness or strength. The word *bound* is used twelve times in the Old Testament, and ten of those times it is translated in the Authorized Version as *prisoner*. Those who are described in the Psalm as being in prison are said to be there:

> *Because they rebelled against the words of God*
> *and contemned the counsel of the Most High.*

The word *contemn*, which is rare in our English language, pictures a people who in spurning, despising, and abhorring the Word of God directed their pathway to a place of incarceration described as being *chained* in *darkness and in the shadow of death.*

The third example is composed of those whom the Psalm describes as Fools. The word *fools* speaks of one who despises wisdom or of one who mocks when shown to be guilty. Because of their transgression, and because of their iniquities, these are afflicted. The word *afflicted* describes one who is busied with, bowed down, or to be depressed.

The fourth example is made up of those who *see the works of the LORD, and his wonders in the deep.* Verses 25 and 26 picture them as being tossed about like a ship caught up in a storm at sea, extremely afraid, and staggering about as if drunk.

Psalm 107:8, 15, 21, and 31 urge the people to thank God for His unfailing love and wonderful deeds. This seems to indicate the advocacy of a prayer style which corresponds to a *fellowship-oriented* style.

Earlier in this study of Habakkuk, two styles of praying were discussed. One style was designated as *circumstance oriented.* The troubled and distressed people had ignored and neglected God until that delinquency brought them into a crisis that put their very existence in jeopardy; then they called upon God for help and deliverance. A look at Psalm 107:6, 13, 19, and 28 will reveal to the reader that the prayers were definitely *circumstance oriented.*

Follow this survey with a similar study of Psalm 107:8, 15, 21, and 31, and it will be learned that the writer is advocating a prayer style that is *fellowship oriented.* A *fellowship oriented* style of praying will help maintain a relationship with God that will guard against the pitfalls that brought others into jeopardy. There is no indication whatsoever that the groups described in the four examples followed a *fellowship oriented* prayer style. On the other hand, it is apparent that the four groups more than likely practiced a *circumstance oriented* prayer style. Their prayers are described as being offered after their troubles developed to a level beyond their ability to manage. It seems rather certain that had they been praying out of a lifestyle of fellowship with God, they would have been directed by God to a lifestyle that would have avoided the pitfalls described.

As we progress through this study of Habakkuk, we will discover the movement from *circumstance oriented* prayer to that of *fellowship oriented* prayer. Habakkuk reveals in chapter 1 verse 2 that he has been praying out of a *circumstance oriented* form. When our study leads us to chapter 3 verse 2, we will learn that the prayer experience has progressed to a *fellowship oriented* prayer form. Here is how he describes it:

> *O LORD, I have heard thy speech, and was afraid:*
> *O LORD, revive thy work in the midst of the years,*
> *in the midst of the years make known; in wrath*
> *remember mercy.*

The desire of this study is for each reader to journey with Habakkuk as he discovers the pathway for this transition. Our study will lead us to revisit these forms of prayer and follow Habakkuk as he experiences a newfound and exciting relationship with God in prayer.

The prophet reveals that he has questions and problems to present to God when he prays. It also seemed to him as if God was not listening. Or, if he were listening, he was not answering.

> *O LORD, how long shall I cry, and thou wilt not*
> *hear! even cry out unto thee of violence, and thou*
> *wilt not save!* (1:2)

But a closer look at the book Habakkuk wrote will reveal some great lessons that he learned when he engaged God in a conversation about his concerns related to prayer.

Before pursuing further any exposition of the content of Habakkuk, we need to see the validity of the preceding line of reasoning. It is readily apparent that Habakkuk is speaking these words with a sense of urgency. It is also to be noticed that there is no pause or otherwise allowance made for God to respond. The result is clearly a monologue. In the conversation, Habakkuk is apparently so intensely involved in the monologue that he fails to recognize that God is both listening and answering his prayer. Habakkuk's prayer is so thoroughly *circumstance-oriented and -driven* that he misunderstands God's action. Habakkuk says that he cried, and God did not listen, hear, or save him. The misdirection of Habakkuk's thinking led him to accuse God of not answering his prayer.

But a closer look at the book Habakkuk wrote will reveal some great lessons that he learned when he engaged God in a conversation about his concerns related to prayer.

The preceding discussion definitely leads to the conclusion that Habakkuk's prayer was *circumstance oriented.* It is rather clear that his attention was riveted securely upon the conditions currently prevailing in the nation of Judah. The focus of his praying was so strongly glued to those conditions that he seems to have lost sight of both the actions and character of God.

Modern-day Believers appear to be afflicted with some form of spiritual eye disease. It may be age-related macular degeneration, cataracts, diabetic retinopathy, glaucoma, or some other disease of the spiritual eyes. Like Habakkuk, we have some kind of vision impairment that prevents a clear view of God and His redemptive activity. As we pursue this study of the prophet Habakkuk, I hope and pray we will learn that it took a very gracious act and strong word from God to redirect the prophet's attention. Study the first response of God recorded in verse 5 for confirmation:

> *Behold ye among the heathen, and regard, and wonder marvelously: for I will work a work in your days, which ye will not believe, though it be told you.*

The dominant word of verse 5 is *behold* (רְאוּ–*ra᾽ ah*). It instructs a person to perceive, to consider. In the intensive form of this verb, it means "to cause to look intently at, behold, cause to gaze at."

A second important word found in this verse is *regard* (וְהַבִּיטוּ–*nabat*), which means "to show regard to, pay attention to, consider."

To the credit of Habakkuk is the degree to which his focus on *circumstances* caused him to realize the contemporary conditions that comprised his view of Judah. We will study those descriptive words as we progress through his conversation with God. The negative aspect of Habakkuk's focus on contemporary circumstances was his simultaneous loss of focus on the God who was controlling both the national events as well as the international events (See the study of verse 6, which comes later). Circumstances blinded the prophet's eyes to God's statement of fact when he said:

> *I will work a work in your days, which ye will not believe, though it be told you.*

I argue not for the removal of the *circumstances* that blinded Habakkuk's eyes to God's activity. Nevertheless, it is true that each Believer needs, and must seek, the divinely assisted development of a Christian worldview that includes both the local scene and the international scene (study Habakkuk 1:5, 6). If and when a Believer's world is so localized that it draws a curtain over the larger view, that person's prayer will become less meaningful and less effective. Such a Christian worldview will allow a focus that will cause the Believer to *wonder marvelously*.

It is hoped that this study of Habakkuk will help us see how God transformed the prophet's myopic worldview. This caused his prayers to change from being *circumstance-oriented and -driven* into a view that brought him to a *fellowship-oriented and -driven* prayer style. This enlarged his concept of God and transformed his prayer style from a monologue of telling God how and when to answer his prayer to a dialogue of conversation with God, which allowed him to understand how God responds to a Believer's prayer.

Chapter Two

A Non-Answer

Habakkuk 1:2-3

O LORD, how long shall I cry, and thou wilt not hear! Even cry out unto thee of violence, and thou wilt not save! Why dost thou shew me iniquity, and cause me to behold grievance? For spoiling and violence are before me: And there are that raise up strife and contention.

Habakkuk 1:2, 3 tells us what inspired the writing of the book. The motivation for the writing of the book comes through in the form of a complaint that is stated in these verses. In the verses Habakkuk indicts God for what he thinks is a refusal to hear and answer a prayer. The matter of *unanswered prayer* is the thesis for the book of Habakkuk. That thesis is the summary of the content of the book bearing his name.

Habakkuk 1:3-4 informs us as to the subject of Habakkuk's prayer in which he indicts God. He says that God is neither listening nor answering his prayer.

> *Why do you show me iniquity, and cause me to behold grievance? For spoiling and violence are before me: And there are that raise up strife and*

contention. Therefore, the law is slacked, and judgment does never go forth: For the wicked do compass about the righteous; Therefore, wrong judgment proceeds.

From this outline of the conversation recorded in the prophecy of Habakkuk, it is rather easy to see that whatever prophecy is contained in the short book is to be found within the context of his conversation with God about prayer.

The book of Habakkuk contains a complaint and the prophet's perception that his prayers were not being heard or answered by God. The book closes with Habakkuk writing a song to God that is both a prayer song and a praise song. Habakkuk has found God to have been faithful in listening and answering his prayers. That is the important thing that we hope to see and understand in this study. From this conversation between Habakkuk and God and the assurance that Habakkuk receives, we are taught so very much about the character and conduct of God and about his response to the prayers of his people.

Habakkuk is classified as a book of prophecy. He is labeled as a minor prophet. However, this study looks at the book for its lessons about prayer. The prophetic element of Habakkuk is considered in this study to be a subject of lesser significance and relevance in the book. Habakkuk is more a book about *prayer* than a book of *prophecy*. Habakkuk does deal with things that are to some extent in the future, but they are discussed during the conversation between Habakkuk and God. And the subject of that conversation is *God's response to Habakkuk's prayer*. Habakkuk is one of the best and most relevant sources of information on prayer, especially so-called unanswered prayers, to be found in the Bible. The Bible records many experiences that persons have had with God in prayer. Abraham interceded for Sodom. Moses interceded for Israel after the gold calf event. Daniel fasted and prayed after reading what Jeremiah wrote about the captivity of Israel. Nehemiah prayed and fasted for three months when one of his "brothers" informed him of the deplorable physical and spiritual conditions of Jerusalem. Jesus prayed in the Garden. Jesus prayed for his disciples (John 17). Paul prayed for the churches he started. But the experience of Habakkuk is one of the most unique and informative of all. Historically Habakkuk has not been considered as the *prophet of prayer* he really was.

Prophecy generally has to do with future events. Habakkuk contains a revelation of future events. The events are in the immediate future for Habakkuk. They reveal some basic principles about the ways in which God deals with people and their sinfulness. In that sense they reveal to us something about how God has acted, is acting, and will act toward sin in our day. But more than it being a revelation of future events, it is an evaluation of information about current prayer experiences. Habakkuk was a *praying prophet*. Prayer is always a contemporary experience. Modern-day people who pray are generally praying about contemporary experiences. These facts combine to constitute Habakkuk as a very contemporary book. It was relevant for the circumstances of his day and it is also relevant for praying people in this day or in any day.

God's people, those who trust in the one true God who made heaven and earth and who in His sovereignty administers its every movement, look to him for some response. They have taken the Bible as their guide for daily living. They are a people of prayer–sincere, earnest prayer, modeled after those great men and women of the Bible. But God sometimes seems not to be responding to their pleas.

The prophet Habakkuk reveals that he had similar questions and problems to present to God as he prayed. It also seemed to him as if God was not listening. Or if He were listening, He was not answering. But a closer look at the book he wrote will reveal some great lessons that he learned when he engaged God in a conversation about his concerns related to unanswered prayer.

Statements made by Habakkuk seem to indicate that he probably lived and ministered during the reign of king Manasseh, when wickedness abounded and destruction was imminent. The Chaldeans, or Babylonians (1:6), whom this prophet mentions, were being used as the instruments of God's judgment. Manasseh was himself carried to Babylon. The reference to the Babylonians (1:6) places the book within the closing years of the seventh century B.C. Precise dating of the prophecy is rather difficult, with dates suggested that are within one of three time periods: the reign of Manasseh (697-642), the reign of Josiah (640-609), and the reign of Jehoiakim (609-598).

The statement made by God recorded in 1:5, "I am going to do something in your day that you would not believe, though it be told you." seems to indicate a time before Babylon's rise as a world power. God is allowing Babylon to ascend to a place of prominence and power among the nations of the world and to become the most dominant power of that era. As a nation of such power, Babylon would conquer Judah and carry most of that nation's citizens and wealth to Babylon, where the nation would serve as slaves for seventy years. This period of history is labeled by the Old Testament scholars as the Babylonian Captivity. Babylon would also be allowed to ransack the temple and destroy Jerusalem. If indeed the fulfillment of Habakkuk's prophecy (1:5) is the fall of Jerusalem at the hands of the Babylonians in 586 B.C, the book would have been written in the middle or later part of Manasseh's reign. That prophecy was to be fulfilled "in your days"-that is, the days of those who heard Habakkuk deliver his prophecy. If they had heard it in the early days of Manasseh, they would probably have died before its fulfillment. This gives us an approximate date for Habakkuk's prophecy as occurring in the last decade of the seventh century B.C.

> *The burden which Habakkuk the prophet did see. O LORD, how long shall I cry, and you will not hear! even cry out unto you of violence, and you will not save! Why do you show me iniquity and cause me to behold grievance? for spoiling and violence are before me: and there are that raise up strife and contention. Therefore, the law is slacked, and judgment does never go forth: for the wicked do compass about the righteous; therefore, wrong judgment proceeds.*

> *Behold you among the heathen, and regard, and wonder marvelously: for I will work a work in your days, which you will not believe, though it be told you. For, lo, I raise up the Chaldeans, that bitter and hasty nation, which shall march through the breadth of the land, to possess the dwelling places that are not theirs. They are terrible and dreadful: their judgment and their dignity shall proceed of themselves. Their horses also are swifter than the leopards and are more fierce than the evening wolves: and their horsemen shall spread themselves, and their horsemen shall come from far; they shall fly as the eagle that hastens to eat. They shall come all for violence: their faces shall sup up as the east wind, and they shall gather the captivity as the sand.*

*And they shall scoff at the kings, and the princes
shall be a scorn unto them: they shall deride every
strong hold; for they shall heap dust and take it.
Then shall his mind change, and he shall pass over,
and offend, imputing this his power unto his god. Art
thou not from everlasting, O LORD my God, mine
Holy One? we shall not die. O LORD, thou hast
ordained them for judgment; and, O mighty God,
thou hast established them for correction. Thou
art of purer eyes than to behold evil, and canst not
look on iniquity: wherefore look you upon them that
deal treacherously, and hold your tongue when the
wicked devours the man that is more righteous than
he? And make men as the fishes of the sea, as the
creeping things, that have no ruler over them? They
take up all of them with the angle, they catch them
in their net, and gather them in their drag: therefore,
they rejoice and are glad. Therefore, they sacrifice
unto their net and burn incense unto their drag;
because by them their portion is fat, and their meat
plenteous. Shall they therefore empty their net, and
not spare continually to slay the nations?*

The opening words of the book of Habakkuk are:

The burden which Habakkuk the prophet did see.
(Habakkuk 1:1).

Habakkuk describes himself as a *prophet* (הַנָּבִיא-*nabi*). In 1
Chronicles 29:29 three words are used for prophet:

Now the acts of David the king, first and last, behold, they are written in the Book of Samuel the Seer (רָאָה–ra-ah) and in the Book of Nathan the prophet (נָבִיא–nabi), and in the Book of Gad the Seer (חֹזֶה–chozeh).

The word הַנָּבִיא (nabi) clearly indicates that the word prophet refers to one who speaks for another. The word for *seer* used in 1 Chronicles 29:29 emphasize the means by which the prophet communicated with God; or maybe we should say, the way God communicated with the prophet. These words give us a definition of the Old Testament prophets as men to whom God communicated a message using such instruments as a vision, and they then became God's spokespersons with the burden of the message upon their hearts and minds to deliver to the people to whom they were sent.

Habakkuk accepts this definition as applying to him and becomes God's servant to share a message with Judah.

The message was called a *burden* by the prophet himself. The nature of its contents created a difficulty in orally delivering it to the people. Having served as a pastor of local congregations for about sixty years, I have learned by experience that there are some messages that weigh so heavily upon the minister's heart that they are hard to deliver and may therefore be classified as burdens. I feel quite certain that any minister who has tried sincerely, faithfully, to thoroughly preach the Word of God will have discovered and can attest to the truth of this statement.

Habakkuk 1:1 speaks of "The burden which Habakkuk the prophet saw." The same two Hebrew words, *burden* and *saw*, are used in Isaiah 13:1: *The burden of Babylon, which Isaiah the son of Amoz did see.* The word *see* (חָזָה–*chazah*) when used by the prophets, often means to see in a vision (Isaiah 1:1, Ezekiel 12:27; Amos 1:1; Micah 1:1). The prophets were sometimes called *seers* because God allowed them to see glimpses of the future. These glimpses were known as *visions.*

What did Habakkuk see? He saw something that birthed in him a very deep and sincere concern for the nation and the people God loved and had chosen for his own. He called it a *burden.* The word *burden* (מַשָּׂא – massa) is used in Proverbs 30:1 and 31:1, where it is translated *prophecy.* By a burden we are to understand the message laid upon the mind of the prophet, and by him pressed on the attention of the people. The message of the Lord is not often regarded as a burden by the people. They too frequently do not feel what the prophet felt so deeply in his heart. But it could not fail to be realized as such by the prophets, who at times felt the weight of their message to be a heavy load.

PRECEPT # 3
To become God's messenger is to learn the real nature of sin.

A passing note is made here about the contents of the burden that Habakkuk saw. The conditions of the world described in the Old Testament book of Habakkuk present us with a striking resemblance to the circumstances and conditions of this century. When one reads the book of Habakkuk, it will be noticed that the political, economic, social, and spiritual events and conditions in Judah all resemble in frightening ways the contemporary conditions. Below is a list of some conditions that Habakkuk saw as constituting his burden. The book of Habakkuk brings these to light very clearly. Habakkuk 1:2-4 contain the prophet's description:

O LORD, how long shall I cry, and thou wilt not hear! even cry out unto thee of violence, and thou wilt not save! Why dost thou shew me iniquity, and cause me to behold grievance? for spoiling and violence are before me: and there are that raise up strife and contention. Therefore the law is slacked, and judgment doth never go forth: for the wicked doth compass about the righteous; therefore wrong judgment proceedeth.

(1) *violence* (v.2)–(חָמָס–*chamac*)–cruelty

(2) *iniquity* (v.3)–(אָוֶן–*aven*)–wicked, mischief

(3) *grievance* (v.3)–(עָמָל - '*amal*)–misery, travail

(4) *spoiling* and violence (v.3)–(שֹׁד - *shod*)–spoiling

(5) strife (v.3)–(רִיב –riyb)–strife

(6) contention (v. 3)–(מָדוֹן–*madown*)–discord

(7) the law is *slacked* (v.4)–(פּוּג–*puwg*)–fainting, feeble

(8) *judgment* does not go forth (v.4)–(מִשְׁפָּט - *mishpat*)–justice, right, lawful

(9) the wicked *compass* the righteous (v.4)–(כָּתַר–kathar)–enclose, surround

(10) *wrong* judgment proceeds (v.4)–(עָקָל - aw·kal)–wrong, distorted

In chapter 2 there are revealed to us five practices that are being followed by the society of Habakkuk's day that bring upon the nation the displeasure of God. They all appear to incorporate the same characteristics of contemporary circumstances. Habakkuk mentions:

(1)   corrupt economic practices (2:6-8),

(2)   greedy financial practices (2:9-11),

(3)   unfair labor practices (2:12-14),

(4)   immoral social practices (2:15-17), and

(5)   ungodly religious practices (2:18-20).

We will look more closely at these as we study the text of Habakkuk's message. All of these conditions and practices are clearly highlighted in Habakkuk.

There is a striking resemblance between the circumstances of the society that Habakkuk describes and the circumstances and conditions of our day.

1.   He saw *violence*–(*chamas*–חָמָס)–The word means "violence; wrong; maliciousness." *Chamas* perhaps connotes a "violent wrongdoing" that has not been righted, the guilt of which lies on the inhabitants of an entire area, disrupting their relationship with God and thereby interfering with His blessings. Has there *ever* been an era more violent than ours?

2.   He saw *strife and contention*–The word *strife* (*rib*–רִיב) appears in the Bible text for the first time in Genesis 26:20: *And the herdmen of Gerar did strive with Isaac's herdmen.* Such "striving" with words is found frequently in the Bible.

The word *contention* (מָדוֹן–*madown*) means "strife, contention, or discord." History records that the period in which we think Habakkuk ministered was one lacking any real peace and tranquility. There was economic, political, social, and spiritual unrest. People were striving with each other, producing a flood of contention. The wise man who wrote Proverbs 6:16–19 had learned that there were some things God actually hated. Here is a list he compiled:

These six things does the LORD hate: yes, seven are an abomination unto him: A proud look, a lying tongue, and hands that shed innocent blood, An heart that devises wicked imaginations, feet that be swift in running to mischief, A false witness that speaks lies, and he that sows discord among brethren.

3. He saw that *the law is slacked*–(*puwg*–תָּפוּג). This is possibly a reference to the difficulty of law enforcement. It carries the idea of being feeble or faint or weak. The *strife* and *contention* produced such disregard for other persons that the laws were broken and could hardly be enforced. The judicial system itself may have become flawed and corrupt, or the officials charged with law enforcement may have defaulted in their responsibility. Or still further the populace may have been in such disarray that law enforcement was difficult.

4. He saw that *judgment does not go forth*–The phrase "does not go forth" (נֶצַח–*netsach*) means movement away from a point." This is a lack of justice. It means that the law is not enforced from the place of established authority. The place for authority in Habakkuk's time was probably the king's throne. That being true, it is implying a national lack of Godly leadership.

5. He saw that the *wicked encompass the righteous*–The prevalence of evil must have seemed to Habakkuk to be growing in the ratio of wicked persons compared to righteous. And wicked deeds were growing at a far more rapid pace than righteousness and were engulfing the righteous. We should remember in this connection the parable Jesus told about the wheat and the tares. The advice of Jesus was: "Do not try to separate them. Let them grow until harvest time. Then the angels will do the separating."

6. He saw that *wrong judgment proceeds*–The word *wrong* (*aqal*–מְעֻקָּל) means "to be bent out of shape, be distorted, be crooked." Justice is perverted. Judicial decisions were not being rendered accurately according to established law and legal precedence. The populace was becoming increasingly dissatisfied with the judicial system. Because of inaccurate decisions by the courts, the people had lost confidence in the judicial system. And they were also quite likely displeased with the executive branch of government—the king.

7. He looked and *behold grievance*–The word *grievance* carries the idea of something difficult, toilsome, and wearisome. People are grieved by evil. They were becoming increasingly dissatisfied with the judicial system. The breakdown of the judicial system had left the public with a distrust for government. This distrust seems not only to have been directed toward the judicial system, but also they were quite likely displeased with the executive branch as well.

The nature of Habakkuk's protest is set out. The setting is apparently about the time of the final Babylonian assault (1:6). Initially Habakkuk's complaint concerns the decline of his own people and culture (1:2-5). He has cried to the Lord for help and expects heaven-sent revival. "How long, O LORD, must I call for help, but you do not listen?" (1:2). His cry seems to indicate that he considered the lack of renaissance in the judicial and social systems to be indicative of God's failure to hear and answer his prayer. The remainder of his complaint lists the symptoms of a culture in disintegration: violence, injustice, wrong, strife, conflict, and the law. God was, in effect, paralyzed.

In summary, there are a few comments to be made concerning Habakkuk's prayer. These things he discovered to be very relevant to effective prayer. So thoroughly did he become convinced about these matters that he gives us some of the most significant truths about prayer to be found in the Bible. I point out these factors here:

1. He talked to God about symptoms rather than causes. The seven actions and attitudes discussed immediately preceding are in reality symptoms rather than causes of the circumstances found in Judah. The symptoms of an issue are the effects of the cause. They are an indication that there is an underlying cause. Habakkuk discovered that his concept of God needed adjusting (1:12ff). He learned that his worldview needed some refinement (1:5).

    His complaint lists the symptoms of a culture in disintegration. So thoroughly did he become convinced about these matters that he gives us some of the most significant truths about prayer to be found in the Bible. He talked to God about symptoms rather than causes. The seven actions and attitudes just mentioned are in reality symptoms rather than causes of the circumstances found in Judah. The symptoms of an issue are the effects of the cause. Much of the turmoil and unrest, etc. which our world is experiencing must be recognized as symptomatic of a cause. The experience of fever or pain illustrates this truth. When a person has an elevated level of fever it is a *symptom* of an infection. Pain is similar in that when a person feels pain it is a *symptom* of an injury of some kind within the body. The application is that when the *symptoms* are discovered about which Habakkuk was praying, the question to ask is *Where is God?*

2.   He learned that in his prayer he had actually been telling God how to answer his prayer. His question "How long?" was tantamount to telling God when to answer. He indicts God as being insensitive to his prayer: "Why dost thou shew me iniquity, and cause me to behold grievance?" (1:3). This statement in chapter one, verse three, was the equivalent of saying that God was not listening and answering his prayer.

In our study we will discover that he hears God's rebuke:

> *For the vision is yet for an appointed time, but at the end it shall speak, and not lie; though it tarry, wait for it; because it will surely come, it will not tarry.* (2:3)

Further analysis of Habakkuk's prayer will come as we proceed with the study of the book.

Chapter Three

O Lord, How Long?

Habakkuk 1:2-4

O LORD, how long shall I cry, and thou wilt not hear! Even cry out unto thee of violence, and thou wilt not save! Why dost thou shew me iniquity, and cause me to behold grievance? For spoiling and violence are before me: And there are that raise up strife and contention. Therefore, the law is slacked, and judgment doth never go forth: For the wicked doth compass about the righteous; Therefore, wrong judgment proceeds.

Our study now leads us to think about *Habakkuk's problem* (Habakkuk 1:2-4). He seemed to conceive of himself as being confronted by an insurmountable difficulty, if not an impossible obstacle. He had begun praying about the deplorable conditions of Judah with strong confidence that God would quickly answer and correct the situation. The absence of an immediate response from God apparently brought Habakkuk to the point of belief that God was not listening and was not going to answer. This conviction of Habakkuk gives birth to what this study perceives as the central issue of the book, namely *God's failure to answer the prophet's prayer.*

39

Habakkuk may register some impatience with God in these words: "O LORD, how long shall I cry, and you will not hear?" But it seems apparent that most of God's people are a bit anxious when it comes to answered prayer. We have not learned how to "wait." Isaiah gives us some very practical words in this regard:

> *But they that wait upon the LORD shall renew their strength; they shall mount up with wings as eagles; they shall run, and not be weary; and they shall walk, and not faint.* (Isaiah 40:31)

PRECEPT # 4
That which is called unanswered prayer is a perception and not a reality.

In the conversation recorded in Habakkuk 1:2-4, the prophet states his problem or complaint:

> *O LORD, how long shall I cry, and you will not hear! even cry out unto you of violence, and you will not save! Why do you show me iniquity and cause me to behold grievance? for spoiling and violence are before me: and there are that raise up strife and contention. Therefore, the law is slacked, and judgment doth never go forth: for the wicked do compass about the righteous; therefore, wrong judgment proceeds.*

The first complaint which was voiced by Habakkuk in his conversation with God is his impatience with God.

O LORD, how long shall I cry, and you will not hear! even cry out unto you of violence, and you will not save! (v.2)

This complaint was voiced in a call to God. A study of the words Habakkuk used to describe his call to God will enable us to better understand just what he was saying to God. He said "I cry" and used a word which means "to cry out (for help) (שָׁוַע–*shava*) or to shout." The second word *cry* is the Hebrew word meaning "to cry out, call for help (זָעַק–*za'aq*)". The emphasis of the first word *cry* is the loudness of the cry. The emphasis of the second word *cry* is the intensity of the cry. It is a reference to what Habakkuk was feeling inside as he prayed.

The first time this word is encountered in the Bible is in the record of the suffering of Israel while in bondage in Egypt: *And the children of Israel sighed by reason of the bondage, and they cried [for help]* (Exodus 2:23). The word (זָעַק–*za'aq*) is most frequently used to indicate the "crying out" for aid in time of emergency, especially *crying out* for divine aid. God often heard this *cry* for help in the time of the judges, as Israel found herself in trouble because of backsliding (Judges 3:9, 15; 6:7; 10:10). The indications are that *za'aq* means "more than a normal speaking volume" by its use in appeals made to the king (2 Samuel 19:28). The word may imply a *crying out* in distress (1 Samuel 4:13), a *cry of horror* (1 Samuel 5:10), or a *cry* of sorrow.

Habakkuk's second complaint to God was the lack of an answer from God. He accused God, saying that he *will not hear*. The audible cry of Habakkuk seems to be inaudible as far as God is concerned. He also said that God *will not save*. The activity of God seems like inactivity as far as Habakkuk is concerned.

The third complaint of Habakkuk was that he, Habakkuk, appeared to experience an increase of trouble. His words to God were:

> *Why do you show me iniquity and cause me to behold grievance? for spoiling and violence are before me: and there are that raise up strife and contention* (v.3).

The word *show* means "to make me see, to inspect, perceive, to consider." Instead of God answering his prayer and causing a decrease in the rampant spread of the spiritual illness that plagued the social structures of Judah. Habakkuk saw the problem as becoming worse and the social structures disintegrating. The word *iniquity* speaks of trouble, wickedness, or sorrow. In using the word *behold*, Habakkuk is asking God to regard, to pay attention, to consider, as if God was unaware of the circumstances of his life and the prevailing conditions of Judah. Habakkuk's use of the word *grievance* implies that God was not informed about the wickedness, toil, labor, and mischief that infected Judah.

But God answers with words Habakkuk probably does not want to hear. Habakkuk wants revival; God promises judgment (1:6-11). If Habakkuk is so concerned about the injustice, he should know that God is going to do something about it: he is going to punish it. God will do something astonishing; he will raise up the Babylonians:

> *that ruthless and impetuous people, who sweep across the whole earth to seize dwelling places not their own* (1:6).

They will come:

bent on violence and *gather prisoners like sand* (1:9).

God does not pretend that the Babylonians are fine folk. After describing the massive strength of their armed forces, he scathingly calls them:

guilty men, whose own strength is their god (1:11).

These guilty men, intoxicated by the ferocity of their own violence, are the people God is going to deploy as instruments to chasten his own covenant people in response to Habakkuk's prayer that God would do something about the injustice in the land.

In the 1960s a period of revival occurred in Indonesia. I had attended seminary with one of our missionaries who, after seminary days, served in Indonesia for fourteen years. When he was back in the States, I listened to him speak of revival in the area where he served. I did not follow through to learn more about what was happening in that part of the world. But in the few years as I began to study Habakkuk, I read something on the Internet about that period of revival. I learned that some books had been published with historical accounts of that revival period. I was led to read that God told Habakkuk to behold (1:5), or to "Look around and see what God was doing in his world." I ordered the books about the revival in Indonesia in the 1960s and read what God did there. I learned that miracles occurred there, which were hard to believe. That experience caused me to consider whether God may say to us: "Look around, discover what is happening in our world—even in the world of unbelievers." God just may be doing something that will cause us to "wonder marvelously." It was, to use a slang expression, like "shock and awe" to me.

The Babylonians (Chaldeans) have been selected by God to be his answer to Habakkuk's prayer.

God's response does not satisfy Habakkuk even if it does go to the heart of the issue. Granted that God is eternal and faithful to his covenant people; granted too that he is *too pure to look on evil* (1:13) and therefore must punish his own covenant community. The burning question remains: "Why then do you tolerate the treacherous? Why are you silent while the wicked swallow up those more righteous than themselves?" (1:13). However wicked the citizens of Judah are, the Babylonians are worse. How can God use the more wicked to punish the less wicked?

God's response (1:5-11) needs to be studied in more detail to enable us to benefit more fully from what he says. The first thing to be seen in God's response is that it is universal (v.5). To say that the response is universal is to say that it is forever contemporary and relevant. God says to Habakkuk: "Behold you among the heathen, and regard, and wonder marvelously: for I will work a work in your days, which you will not believe, though it be told you."

God first tells Habakkuk to *Behold. (ra>ah–רְאוּ)* The word used means "to see, observe, perceive, get acquainted with, gain understanding, examine, look after (see to), choose, discover." Basically *ra>ah* connotes seeing with one's eyes. Habakkuk, you remember, has complained that God is not listening to, hearing, and answering his prayer. God in response asks Habakkuk to open his eyes and observe what is happening in the nations of the world of his day.

That would seem to be a wise and profitable exercise for the twenty-first-century Believer.

God tells Habakkuk to *Behold you among the heathen.* The use of the word *heathen* (*goyim*-בַּגּוֹיִם) is interesting. A very simple definition of this word is that it refers to all non-Jewish people of Habakkuk's world. It often represents a group of individuals who are considered as a unit with respect to origin, language, land, jurisprudence, and government. It is sometimes almost a derogatory name for non-Israelite groups. The *heathen* refers to all non-Jewish people. Evidence of God's activity among the non-Jewish nations of the world could be easily seen if Habakkuk would but open his eyes and look. God is instructing Habakkuk to *behold*, or to conduct a survey of, events taking place among the non-Jewish nations of the world and realize that what is happening is definitely of divine origin and intent.

In summary, God is saying to Habakkuk: "If you would only open your eyes and look at what is happening in the nations of your world you would see and understand that I have heard your prayers and am actively in the process of answering them."

Habakkuk is warned by God that he would see a unique response. God uses the words *wonder marvelously* (תָּמַהּ–taw·mah) "to be in consternation, be amazed, be astonished" (v.5), to describe what Habakkuk would see. The idea connoted by these words is to be astonished, to be stunned, amazed, dumbfounded.

PRECEPT # 5
Sensitivity in prayer causes a person to "wonder marvelously."

Long before Habakkuk was informed by God about how the work God had planned would cause him to *wonder marvelously*, God had said through Isaiah that he would do such an amazing work. In Isaiah 29:14, God said:

> *Therefore, behold, I will proceed to do a marvelous work among this people, Even, a marvelous work and a wonder: For the wisdom of their wise men shall perish, And the understanding of their prudent men shall be hid.*

In Acts 13:41 we read about Elymas, a sorcerer, who opposed Paul and Barnabas as they were teaching. Paul, in defense of the gospel, quoted this idea from Habakkuk, and said to the crowd:

> *Behold, ye despisers, and wonder, and perish, for I work a work in your days, a work which ye shall in no wise believe, though a man declare it unto you.*

Habakkuk could not detect and discern the way of God in answering prayer. His cry, recorded in Habakkuk 1:2, was:

> *O LORD, how long shall I cry, and thou wilt not hear! Even cry out unto thee of violence, and thou wilt not save!*

Because of this flaw in his prayer life, Habakkuk was left with only the recourse of complaining about God's failure to answer his praying. He should have somehow learned about Elijah's praying. James describes it in James 5:13-18:

> *Is any among you afflicted? let him pray. Is any merry? let him sing psalms. Is any sick among you? let him call for the elders of the church; and let them pray over him, anointing him with oil in the name of the Lord: And the prayer of faith shall save the sick, and the Lord shall raise him up; and if he have committed sins, they shall be forgiven him. Confess your faults one to another, and pray one for another, that ye may be healed. The effectual fervent prayer of a righteous man availeth much. Elias was a man subject to like passions as we are, and he prayed earnestly that it might not rain: and it rained not on the earth by the space of three years and six months. And he prayed again, and the heaven gave rain, and the earth brought forth her fruit.*

Generations after Habakkuk struggled to find assurance that God could and had answered his prayer, the writer of Romans 11:33-36 exclaimed:

> O *the depth of the riches both of the wisdom and knowledge of God! how unsearchable are his judgments, and his ways past finding out! For who hath known the mind of the Lord? or who hath been his counselor? Or who hath first given to him, and it shall be recompensed unto him again? For of him, and through him, and to him, are all things: to whom be glory forever. Amen.* (Romans 11:33-36).

Habakkuk had complained that God, instead of listening to his prayer, has made him to look at the exceeding sinfulness of his nation and world. Here both the prophet and the people are found to suffer from a severe case of myopia. They were very nearsighted. God is asking them to get their eyes off the dark, bleak conditions that characterize the nation and look at the larger picture. He instructs them to develop a Biblical worldview. They needed to see what was happening among the *heathen—the nations*. When the larger picture fills their vision, they will be utterly amazed by what they discover. That which God is doing and is about to do will cause them to *wonder marvelously*. God is involved in, and He is indeed in control of, the contemporary worldwide events, and He is about to do a work that will be hard for them to believe, even though they will be assured that it is God who is doing it.

Forgive a brief negative word. It seems that much of our praying consists of telling God what answer we expect. Added to that, we also tell Him what time we expect the answer to come. Habakkuk seemed to experience a similar approach to prayer. That attitude prompted his complaint about God's process of answering. It would be a great advantage, one would think, if we could make a request of God without having it compromised by a preconceived idea as to how and when it must be answered. This would eliminate much confusion and disappointment on the part of the intercessor. God spoke through Isaiah relative to this matter in chapter 65:24, saying:

> *And it shall come to pass, that before they call, I will answer; and while they are yet speaking, I will hear.*

Again, Isaiah wrote some very practical words to God's people in chapter 40:28-31:

> *Have you not known? have you not heard, that the everlasting God, the LORD, the Creator of the ends of the earth, faints not, neither is weary? there is no searching of his understanding. He gives power to the faint; and to them that have no might he increases strength. Even the youths shall faint and be weary, and the young men shall utterly fall: But they that wait upon the LORD shall renew their strength; they shall mount up with wings as eagles; they shall run, and not be weary; and they shall walk, and not faint.*

And when God's messenger came to inform Daniel as to the response being made to his prayer, Daniel learned a great lesson relative to this matter. In Daniel 10 the story is related. After a prolonged period of fasting and praying, prompted by Daniel's discovery of Jeremiah's prophecy about the seventy years of captivity, he saw a vision of the pre-incarnate Christ. And he recounts the experience for us in verses 10-14:

> *And, behold, a hand touched me, which set me upon my knees and upon the palms of my hands. And he said unto me, O Daniel, a man greatly beloved, understand the words that I speak unto you, and stand upright: for unto you am I now sent. And when he had spoken this word unto me, I stood trembling. Then said he unto me, Fear not, Daniel: for from the first day that you did set your heart to understand, and to chasten yourself before*

*your God, your words were heard, and I am come
for your words. But the prince of the kingdom of
Persia withstood me one and twenty days: but, lo,
Michael, one of the chief princes, came to help
me; and I remained there with the kings of Persia.
Now I am come to make you understand what shall
befall your people in the latter days: for yet the
vision is for many days.*

Notice in Daniel 10:12 how he was informed that from the first
day of his period of fasting and prayer God had heard and dispatched a messenger to communicate the answer to Daniel. The
messenger was delayed by the prince of the kingdom of Persia,
who withstood the messenger for twenty-one days. With the aid
of Michael, a chief prince, the messenger had been released to
deliver the answer to Daniel.

God's people sometimes seem to be very slow learners. The preceding quoted passage from the book of Daniel grows out of an
experience Daniel had while reading and studying the book of
Jeremiah. Yet Daniel had not learned what Jeremiah had written
about God's answering the prayers of his people. He had prayed so
intensely and relevantly about Judah's coming captivity in Babylon.
But God had to miraculously appear to him to get the message
through to him that his prayer was answered from the moment he
began to pray. God had given these words in Jeremiah 29:11-14:

*For I know the thoughts that I think toward you,
saith the LORD, thoughts of peace, and not of
evil, to give you an expected end. Then shall you
call upon me, and you shall go and pray unto me,
and I will hearken unto you And you shall seek me,*

and find me, when you shall search for me with all
your heart. And I will be found of you, saith the
LORD: and I will turn away your captivity, and
I will gather you from all the nations, and from
all the places whither I have driven you, saith the
LORD; and I will bring you again into the place
whence I caused you to be carried away captive.

In Habakkuk 1:5-11 God interrupts Habakkuk's accusatory complaint to inform him that he has, in fact, both heard the *cry* and
initiated the appropriate response. It is made quite clear in God's
words to Habakkuk that he, and no doubt the entire nation of Judah,
needs an informed Biblical worldview. The nation has become so
steeped in its rejection of God's laws that it is extremely self-centered, selfish, and self-serving and cannot see the larger picture of
what God is doing throughout the world. It is more than clearly
revealed that the prophet himself is very deficient in this area. God
has chosen him to be His spokesperson in the last days before the
nation of Judah is deported to Babylon, but he is so nearsighted
that he does not understand what God is up to in His world. This
fact has governed Habakkuk's cry and complaint to God.

PRECEPT # 6
Prayer reveals God's plan of action.

God reveals to Habakkuk that which He is going to do, and
Habakkuk finds it is a totally unexpected action:

For, lo, I raise up the Chaldeans, that bitter and
hasty nation, which shall march through the
breadth of the land, to possess the dwelling places
that are not theirs. They are terrible and dreadful:

their judgment and their dignity shall proceed of themselves. Their horses also are swifter than the leopard and are more fierce than the evening wolves: and their horsemen shall spread themselves, and their horsemen shall come from far; they shall fly as the eagle that hastens to eat. They shall come all for violence: their faces shall sup up as the east wind, and they shall gather the captivity as the sand. And they shall scoff at the kings, and the princes shall be a scorn unto them: they shall deride every strong hold; for they shall heap dust and take it. Then shall his mind change, and he shall pass over, and offend, imputing this his power unto his god. (Hab. 1:6-11)

These verses indicate a wonderful truth about God responding to our prayers. God is absolutely sovereign over this world and all that is in it. Nothing ever happens in this world that is not caused or permitted by God. There are no surprises with God. He already knows. This fact should magnify God in our minds and hearts. The greatness of God cannot be overstated. He is *Lord of heaven and earth.*

A second truth, which is presented by implication, serves as the foundation to the basic one and has to do with the nature of God. The truth is that when a member of the family of God prays, they cannot dictate to God just how or when to answer. Nor can that person predict with any degree of accuracy just what form the answer will take. Habakkuk had no idea and no expectation that the answer to his prayer would be the judging of Judah. He had not the faintest idea that the nation of Babylon would be God's instrument with which to answer his prayer. Praying with a preplanned answer or a preconceived picture of what the answer will be or how it will be delivered will create a heart fixation that will make it difficult if not impossible to recognize the answer when it comes. And too, it will facilitate the attitude of disappointment and complaint in the experience of what is thought to be a non-answer. For this reason, the Scriptures exhort us to wait on the Lord. In fact, the Scriptures are replete with exhortations for God's family to wait patiently on the Lord.

The exhortation of Philippians 4:4-7 is very apropos:

> *Rejoice in the Lord always: and again, I say, Rejoice. Let your moderation be known unto all men. The Lord is at hand. Be careful for nothing; but in everything by prayer and supplication with thanksgiving let your requests be made known unto God. And the peace of God, which passes all understanding, shall keep your hearts and minds through Christ Jesus.*

A friend once gave this summary statement of these verses:

> *Don't worry about anything; Pray about everything; Tell God what you want; and don't forget to thank him in advance for his answer.*

Chapter Four

Surprise!

Habakkuk 1:5-17

Behold you among the heathen, and regard, and wonder marvelously: For I will work a work in your days, Which you will not believe, though it be told you. For, lo, I raise up the Chaldeans, that bitter and hasty nation, Which shall march through the breadth of the land, To possess the dwelling places that are not theirs. They are terrible and dreadful: Their judgment and their dignity shall proceed of themselves. Their horses also are swifter than the leopards And are more fierce than the evening wolves: And their horsemen shall spread themselves, And their horsemen shall come from far; They shall fly as the eagle that hastens to eat. They shall come all for violence: Their faces shall sup up as the east wind, And they shall gather the captivity as the sand. And they shall scoff at the kings, And the princes shall be a scorn unto them: They shall deride every strong hold; or they shall heap dust and take it. Then shall his mind change, and he shall pass over, and offend, Imputing this his power unto his god.

*Are you not from everlasting, O L*ORD *my God, my Holy One? we shall not die. O L*ORD*, you have ordained them for judgment; And, O mighty God, you have established them for correction. You are of purer eyes than to behold evil, And cannot look on iniquity: Wherefore look you upon them that deal treacherously, And hold your tongue when the wicked devours the man that is more righteous than he? And make men as the fishes of the sea, As the creeping things, that have no ruler over them? They take up all of them with the angle, They catch them in their net, and gather them in their drag: Therefore they rejoice and are glad. Therefore they sacrifice unto their net, and burn incense unto their drag; Because by them their portion is fat, and their meat plenteous. Shall they therefore empty their net, And not spare continually to slay the nations?*

Behold you among the heathen, and regard, and wonder marvelously.

"**B**ehold" (רָאָה–*ra'ah*). According to the *Enhanced Strong's Lexicon*, this word means "to see" by use of the perception of sight to view objects and make judgments based on the perceptions. It is also used meaning "to find out or discover or to learn information about a situation or object by testing or by observation."

Then there's *among the heathen* (גּוֹיִם–goyim). This word is usually to reference non-Hebrew people. God appears to be telling Habakkuk to carefully look at and make decisions and judgments based upon the recent and current events taking place among the non-Jewish people of his world.

God tells Habakkuk that when he has come to an objective, unbiased opinion about what is happening in his world, he will *wonder marvelously*. The word used here is translated in the KJV (and others) by these two words: *wonder marvelously*. The Hebrew word *tā·mǎh* (תָּמַהּ) is transporting the idea "to be astonished, be astounded, be stunned, or to be in a state or condition of surprise as a reaction to a situation."

PRECEPT # 7
Sensitive prayer discloses God's nature.

Several factors can be found that would cause *surprise* and cause Habakkuk to *wonder marvelously*.

One would be God's use of Babylon (the Chaldeans) as his instrument of judgment on Judah. As we will discuss that nation is described as being *bitter* and *hasty*.

> *For, lo, I raise up the Chaldeans, that bitter and hasty nation, which shall march through the breadth of the land, to possess the dwelling places that are not theirs. (1:6)*

Another would be the nature of Babylon. Habakkuk describes that nation (the one used to judge) as being more sinful than Judah (the nation being judged).

> *You are of purer eyes than to behold evil, and cannot look on iniquity: wherefore look you upon*

> *them that deal treacherously, and hold your tongue*
> *when the wicked devours the man that is more*
> *righteous than he?* (1:13)

Three would be the strength of Babylon. Babylon had grown rapidly into a nation known worldwide for its military prowess.

> *Are you not from everlasting, O LORD my God, my*
> *Holy One? we shall not die. O LORD, you have*
> *ordained them for judgment; And, O mighty God,*
> *you have established them for correction. You are*
> *of purer eyes than to behold evil, And cannot look*
> *on iniquity: Wherefore look you upon them that*
> *deal treacherously, And hold your tongue when*
> *the wicked devours the man that is more righteous*
> *than he? And make men as the fishes of the sea, As*
> *the creeping things, that have no ruler over them?*
> *They take up all of them with the angle, They catch*
> *them in their net, and gather them in their drag:*
> *Therefore they rejoice and are glad. Therefore,*
> *they sacrifice unto their net, and burn incense*
> *unto their drag; Because by them their portion is*
> *fat, and their meat plenteous. Shall they therefore*
> *empty their net, And not spare continually to slay*
> *the nations?* (1:12-17)

Four would be the character of God. Habakkuk thought God was acting contrary to his own character in using Babylon, the more sinful nation, to judge Judah, the less sinful nation.

> *Are you not from everlasting, O LORD my God, my*
> *Holy One? we shall not die. O LORD, you have*

ordained them for judgment; And, O mighty God, you have established them for correction. You are of purer eyes than to behold evil, And cannot look on iniquity: Wherefore look you upon them that deal treacherously, And hold your tongue when the wicked devours the man that is more righteous than he? (1:12-13)

It seems that Habakkuk did not expect God to choose and use the Chaldeans as the instrument of judgment. But God had predetermined to use unexpected sources—the Chaldeans or Babylon—to bring to pass his answer to Habakkuk's prayer. This study will refer to the nation as Babylon because that is the more familiar designation.

The element of prophecy enters the book of Habakkuk in 1:6. At this point Habakkuk is introduced to the idea that God is using the nation of Babylon to bring judgment upon Judah. Prophecy seems to generally impose a new, or at least a fresh, factor into the equation of world events. And this makes prophecy such an interesting study. It also creates pause for us to comprehend just what God is revealing. Habakkuk strains at the concept of God using such a nation as the up-and-coming kingdom of Babylon. And that leads him to interrupt God and make his now classic statement recorded in 1:12-17 about God's character as he perceives it.

God describes the nation of Babylon (the Chaldeans) as a *bitter* people. The word for *bitter* is the same word that is used to describe the water about which Israel voiced their complaint when they were on the way to Canaan (Exodus 15:23). As a description of the nation, the word probably is intended to indicate that the harsh, warlike activities of Babylon left the other nations feeling bitter.

The Babylonians were also a *hasty* people. There is an apparent intentional play on words found here. The word for *hasty* is *mahar* (וְהַנִּמְהָר) and the word for *bitter* is *mar* (מַר). The reading of the Hebrew text has God describing them as *mar* and *mahar* (bitter and hasty).

God indicates that He will *raise* up the nation of Babylon. Babylon's rise as a world power came to the forefront in 612B.C, when the armies of Babylon overthrew Nineveh. But the battle of Carchemish in 605B.C, when Nebuchadnezzar defeated Pharaoh Neco II of Egypt, actually marks the date when Babylon became a force to be reckoned with. The nation quickly rose to become a formidable nation making its bid for world power.

God's revelation that he is using Babylon brings with it his description of that nation. That description is found in 1:6-11. It is quite revealing. It is given in order that we might get a better concept of the significance of God's choice of Babylon as His instrument to administer judgment upon Judah. Consider the conversation between God and Habakkuk in this fashion.

Babylon is described from the viewpoint of the nation being God's instrument to administer judgment upon Judah. After God gives a brief description of Babylon in 1:6-11, Habakkuk makes his classic statement about God's character. Included in Habakkuk's statement is his own description of Babylon. His description seems to view the nation from the perspective of its effect upon the citizens of Judah and upon himself. There is a marked distinction between the way God views Babylon and the way Habakkuk sees that wicked nation. These two viewpoints will be seen as we move consecutively through the verses of this prophecy. The conversation about prayer and God's method of responding to the prayer of His prophet will be highlighted.

Isaiah wrote several centuries before Habakkuk voiced his prayer and complaint. In chapter 43:14-21, Isaiah prophesied that God *had* brought judgment upon Babylon. Isaiah uses the past tense, even though the event is to happen many years in the future. Read again Isaiah's prophecy:

> *This is what the* LORD, *your redeemer, the Holy One of Israel, says; For your sake I have sent to Babylon, And have brought down all their nobles, And the Chaldeans, whose cry is in the ships. I am the* LORD, *your Holy One, The creator of Israel, your King. This is what the* LORD *says, which makes a way in the sea, And a path in the mighty waters; Which brings forth the chariot and horse, the army and the power; They shall lie down together, they shall not rise: They are extinct, they are quenched as tow. Remember you not the former things, Neither consider the things of old. Behold, I will do a new thing; Now it shall spring forth; shall you not know it? I will even make a way in the wilderness, And rivers in the desert. The beast of the field shall honor me, The dragons and the owls: Because I give waters in the wilderness, And rivers in the desert, To give drink to my people, my chosen. This people have I formed for myself; They shall shew forth my praise.*

In the next chapters (44:28-45:3), Isaiah prophesies that later on in the history of Babylon Cyrus will become ruler of Persia. Persia was to be the nation of God's choice to bring judgment upon Babylon. Isaiah tells us about God choosing Cyrus, his name, his future performance, and his future position as king. Isaiah reveals this about Cyrus:

> *That says of Cyrus, He is my shepherd, and shall perform all my pleasure: even saying to Jerusalem, You, shall be built; and to the temple, Your, foundation shall be laid. Thus says the LORD to his anointed, to Cyrus, whose right hand I have held, to subdue nations before him; and I will lose the loins of kings, to open before him the two leaved gates; and the gates shall not be shut; I will go before you, and make the crooked places straight: I will break in pieces the gates of brass, and cut in sunder the bars of iron: And I will give you the treasures of darkness, and hidden riches of secret places, that you may know that I, the LORD, which call you by your name, am the God of Israel.*

Now here is the application of Isaiah's prophecy. First, remember this: Daniel was reading Jeremiah's prophecy of the Babylonian captivity of Judah. It moved him to an extended period of prayer and fasting. He, not unlike Habakkuk, had trouble with the delay of God's answer to his prayer. But God sent His messenger, who revealed to Daniel that God had actually answered his prayer when it was first offered. The messenger informed Daniel that another spiritual battle had delayed him in delivering the answer. The question to ask as we read Habakkuk's complaint is, "Why did Habakkuk not know about God's delay in answering Daniel's prayer?"

There are four great and clear reasons he should have known:

1. Habakkuk should have known the prophecies of Isaiah.

2. Daniel should have discovered the prophecies of Isaiah as he did those of Jeremiah.

3. Habakkuk probably should have known the prophecies of Jeremiah.

4. Habakkuk should have known about Daniel's experience.

Habakkuk is thought to have been the latest of these four prophets (Habakkuk, Isaiah, Jeremiah, and Daniel). Therefore, it can be reasoned that he should have known the prophetic content of the other three. Why did he not know? Yes. The answer can only be speculation. But it can be rather strong speculation. Ask the follow-up -the application- questions:

- Why do we not know that God always answers prayer?

- Why do we find it so hard to look around and see God at work?

- Why do we find it so very difficult to learn to "wait upon the Lord"?

- Why do we not know that we cannot-therefore we must not-tell God how and when to answer our prayers?

- Why is our prayer so often the same as the prayer of Habakkuk:

O LORD, how long shall I cry, and you will not hear?

Chapter Five

Behold!

Habakkuk 1:5-17

Behold you among the heathen, and regard, and wonder marvelously: for I will work a work in your days, which you will not believe, though it be told you. For, lo, I raise up the Chaldeans, that bitter and hasty nation, which shall march through the breadth of the land, to possess the dwelling places that are not theirs. They are terrible and dreadful: their judgment and their dignity shall proceed of themselves. Their horses also are swifter than the leopards and are more fierce than the evening wolves: and their horsemen shall spread themselves, and their horsemen shall come from far; they shall fly as the eagle that hastens to eat. They shall come all for violence: their faces shall sup up as the east wind, and they shall gather the captivity as the sand. And they shall scoff at the kings, and the princes shall be a scorn unto them: they shall deride every strong hold; for they shall heap dust and take it. Then shall his mind change, and he shall pass over, and offend, imputing this his power unto his god.

Are you not from everlasting, O LORD my God, mine Holy One? we shall not die. O LORD, you have ordained them for judgment; and, O mighty God, you have established them for correction. You are of purer eyes than to behold evil, and cannot look on iniquity: wherefore look you upon them that deal treacherously, and hold your tongue when the wicked devours the man that is more righteous than he? And make men as the fishes of the sea, as the creeping things, that have no ruler over them? They take up all of them with the angle, they catch them in their net, and gather them in their drag: therefore, they rejoice and are glad. Therefore, they sacrifice unto their net and burn incense unto their drag; because by them their portion is fat, and their meat plenteous. Shall they therefore empty their net, and not spare continually to slay the nations?

God will use unexpected means-the lawless, swift, violent mockery of the godless-to answer our prayers. God can and may be using the terrorists of our day. God's people, then and now, find it difficult to see and believe that He can and does use nations and/or individual persons who are totally nonbelievers to accomplish His purposes of discipline, chastening, and saving those whom He has chosen as His own. Habakkuk is about to learn that God in His wisdom and sovereignty has and still does use such instrumentality. There is a real need for all Believers to read and reread from the prophets, especially such passages as that quoted in the previous chapter from Isaiah 44:28 to 45:3, to understand more fully and clearly the way God works.

For example, observe how he used Egypt and the period of bondage to save and develop Israel. Read and study carefully passages such as Exodus 9:13-6:

> *And the LORD said unto Moses, Rise up early in the morning, and stand before Pharaoh, and say unto him, This, is what the LORD God of the Hebrews says, 'Let my people go, that they may serve me. For I will at this time send all my plagues upon your heart, and upon your servants, and upon your people; that you may know that there is none like me in all the earth. For now, I will stretch out my hand that I may smite you and your people with pestilence; and you shall be cut off from the earth. And in very deed for this cause have I raised you up, for to show in you my power; and that my name may be declared throughout all the earth.*

We do not normally expect such ungodly persons or nations to be God's instruments. But God, throughout recorded history, used them in rather profound ways. God is asking Habakkuk to look around and see His work in progress (1:5). Habakkuk is told that he will be amazed and *wonder marvelously* when he sees how God is currently at work and when it is discovered to him what God has planned to do for, with, and to his own life and that of his nation.

Contemporary believers, especially those who engage God in prayer, must be vigilant to see God at work, and sensitive to discern what God is doing in response to prayer. Habakkuk accused God of failure to listen to and answer his prayer because he was neither vigilant nor sensitive to what God was doing. In verses 5-11 Habakkuk seems not to be vigilant and therefore fails to observe God's *works* in his world. In verses 12-17 he seems not to be sensitive and so he does not recognize that contemporary events are the direct result of the work of God who is holy, just, pure, eternal, and the creator and sustainer of the universe in which he lives.

On the video titled *A Billy Graham Homecoming, Vol. 1*, Bill Gaither records Beverly Shea telling the history of how he came into possession of the hymn "How Great Thou Art." He also tells how some of the lyrics that we now sing came into being. Mr. Shea met Mr. George Gray on Oxford Street in London one afternoon in 1954. Mr. Gray handed Mr. Shea a copy of the song, including the translation into English. Bev Shea got together with Cliff Barrow, and they read the lyrics of the song. As Bev Shea read the first lines of the lyrics of the hymn, he came to the line, "O Lord my God! When I in awesome wonder Consider all the works Thy hand have made." He wanted it to read, "Consider all the 'worlds' Thy hands have made." In similar fashion, upon reading the following line–"I see the stars, I hear the mighty thunder Thy power throughout the universe displayed"–Bev Shea wanted to sing, "I hear the 'rolling' thunder." The two of them got in touch with the translator of the song, Mr. Hine, and gained permission to make the changes in the translation.

I tell this story to emphasize the vigilance prerequisite to seeing God's handiwork and the sensitivity necessary to understand God's reason for doing what He is doing. Vigilance opens the eyes to see *what* God is doing and sensitivity enables the mind to understand *why* God is doing what He does. Habakkuk seemed to be lacking in both. So he indicted God for not listening and answering his prayer.

Ezekiel also spoke relative to the fall of Israel and Jerusalem. In Ezekiel 25-32 the number of nations that come under the condemnation of God is seven: Ammon, Moab, Edom, Philistia, Tyre, Sidon, and Egypt. Ezekiel's statements about these seven nations may have been uttered over an extended span of Ezekiel's ministry, but their gathering in this way into seven, and only seven, suggests that the number itself is symbolic. God instructs Habakkuk to "Behold among the heathen..." (1:5). God speaks to all the nations. Worthy of note is the fact that Babylon is not included on Ezekiel's list. That may be due to the fact that Babylon is to be God's agent in crushing all of these nations. The first twenty-four chapters of Ezekiel outline clearly God's planned action for these nations. But before revealing the results of God's actions, Ezekiel prophesies what will be experienced by all these nations. Then Ezekiel reveals what has happened to Jerusalem.

The first four nations on the list contained in Ezekiel 25 are small entities that surround Israel. It appears that Babylon conquered these nations before the attack on Jerusalem. But when the army of Babylon laid siege and ultimately destroyed Jerusalem and Judah, these four joined in the final assault. They may have been trying to curry the favor of Babylon. But more than likely they were also trying to demolish Judah. Their heartless gloating and arrogant vengeance is an abomination to the Lord, and they will pay for it. Reflect on the implications of this truth.

Let us continue our review of God's description of Babylon. We resume our study beginning at 1:7:

They are terrible and dreadful: their judgment and their dignity shall proceed of themselves.

The idea in the word *terrible* (אָיֹם -ʾ*ayom*) is based upon a Hebrew root that means "to frighten." Babylon is not only a *bitter* and *hasty* and *terrible* nation, but we are given a third reason why the nation was to be such a powerful instrument of judgment: the nation was also *dreadful*. The word (*yare*–וְנוֹרָא) means "to be afraid, stand in awe, or fear." Other nations had apparently developed a fear of Babylon because of her harsh treatment of conquered nations.

Those who offer prayer to God sometime seem to be a bit hasty in framing the prayer. There are surrounding factors that cause such haste in making the request. Babylon's reputation caused the surrounding nations to experience great fear. She was a *dreadful* nation. Sometime our requests are framed in the light of personal perception, personal preference, and personal performance.

A contributing factor in the development of that fear was that Babylon had become its own law:

> *Their judgment and their dignity shall proceed of themselves.*

The word *judgment* (*mishpat*–מִשְׁפָּטוֹ) has two main ideas: the first deals with the act of sitting as a judge, hearing a case, and rendering a proper verdict. The other is a reference to the *rights* belonging to someone. This may suggest that Babylon recognized no international code of conduct such as the Geneva Conventions, under which modern nations operate. The Geneva Conventions are rules that apply only in times of armed conflict and seek to protect people who are not, or are no longer, taking part in hostilities. This includes the sick and wounded of the armed forces on the field of battle; wounded, sick, and shipwrecked members of the armed forces at sea; prisoners of war; and civilians. Babylon decided within herself what the code would be that governed the actions of a nation bent on conquest, as she was.

God then tells Habakkuk that the things he has mentioned as characteristic of Babylon are a source of national pride. The word in the KJV is *dignity.* The word speaks of elevation, exaltation, dignity, swelling, and uprising. Babylon was a self-centered, selfish, sinful nation, and was just plainly proud.

The nation also possessed considerable military strength. God's description is:

> *Their horses also are swifter than the leopards and are more fierce than the evening wolves: and their horsemen shall spread themselves, and their horsemen shall come from far; they shall fly as the eagle that hastens to eat. They shall come all for violence: their faces shall sup up as the east wind, and they shall gather the captivity as the sand.* (Habakkuk 1:8–9)

Conjoined with the pride of Babylon was her military strength. The leaders of the conquered nations were ridiculed and mocked. The cities of the nations that had been fortified against military attack were derided before they were conquered by Babylon. Listen to how God describes the scene:

> *And they shall scoff at the kings, and the princes shall be a scorn unto them: they shall deride every strong hold; for they shall heap dust and*

*take it. Then shall his mind change, and he shall
pass over, and offend.* (Habakkuk 1:9–11)

The last characteristic that made Babylon such an effective
instrument for God's use in bringing judgment upon Judah
was her godlessness. Habakkuk 1:11 says that Babylon was
"imputing this his power unto his god." Some scholars see this
statement as saying that Babylon's power was her god. Such
power as God describes belonging to Babylon is indeed a heady
thing, and that nation seems to have made it her god. This, at
least in part, is why God's people of any period of time need
to cultivate a biblical worldview. Doing so will help prevent
surprise and misunderstanding about whatever method God
chooses to accomplish his purposes. Our nation, for example,
must be careful that in her greatness and strength as perhaps
militarily the strongest nation in the contemporary world, that
strength does not become her god and from that gain a sense of
being invincible. Such power as that which Habakkuk describes
as belonging to Babylon seems always to birth a corresponding
sense of independence and arrogance.

Habakkuk saw an increase of trouble and thought it to be
God's response:

*Why do you show me iniquity and cause me to
behold grievance? for spoiling and violence are
before me: and there are that raise up strife and
contention.* (Habakkuk 1:3, 4)

He asked: "Why do you show me iniquity?" The word for
show is (*ra›ah*–רָאָה) and means "to see, observe, perceive,
get acquainted with, gain understanding, examine." Basically

ra̓ah connotes seeing with one's eyes. Habakkuk seems to be accusing God of deliberately allowing him to visually look upon the awful iniquity taking place around him while he remained helpless to reduce the flow. The perception that prayer is not heard and answered creates an inner sense of weakness.

The word for *iniquity* is (אָוֶן–*'aven*) which in a deeper sense characterizes the way of life of those who are without God. Though all people have this infection, there are those who delight in causing difficulties and *misfortunes* for others by scheming, lying, and deception. Those who are actively involved, intentionally or otherwise, in the ways of darkness are called the "workers of iniquity," the doers of evil or the creators of *misfortune* and disaster. They are seen as being opposed to *righteousness* and *justice*. They seek the downfall of the just.

God instructs Habakkuk to *behold* (*nabat*–נָבַּ) this. The word means "to look, regard, behold." While *nabat* is commonly used for physically *looking* (Exodus 3:6), the word is frequently used metaphorically to mean a spiritual and inner apprehension.

The verb used here is in the Hebrew tense (*hiphil*), which corresponds generally to an English passive-voice verb and means "to cause to behold." Habakkuk seems to accuse God not only of allowing him to see the abundance of iniquity but of actually causing him to look on the horrible activity taking place.

God is also accused of causing Habakkuk to look at *grievance* (*amal*–עָמָל). The reference is to "labor; toil; anguish; troublesome work; trouble; misery." The word means "to labor" in the sense of toil. It can also mean "troublesome work" with the emphasis on the difficulty involved in a task or work as troublesome and burdensome. Again, *amal* can have an ethical connotation and is used as a word for sin.

The word *grievance* from the Hebrew of the Old Testament does not mean the same as our English word. Our word carries the idea of a complaint, a mistreatment, or a misapplication of rules of engagement. The Hebrew word connotes the effect of an activity. As used here it speaks of the horror and hurt of rampant sin. It has to do with the *grievousness* of sin.

And last, God is seen as causing Habakkuk to witness a failure of the laws of society:

> *Therefore, the law is slacked, and judgment does never go forth: for the wicked do compass about the righteous; therefore, wrong judgment proceeds.* (Habakkuk 1:4)

The phrase "the law is slacked" actually means that the law is ignored. The law is permitted to grow numb, feeble, faint. A part of the effect of sin was a weakening of law enforcement.

Not only was the law *slack*; there was also *wrong judgment*. The meaning is that the laws were perverted. The reference is to the act of making the wrong decision in deciding a case. When the judicial system of a nation fails to function properly, or when it functions in a perverted way, the entire population suffers from an acceleration of lawless activity. Ecclesiastes 8:11 speaks relevantly to this subject when it says: "Because sentence against an evil work is not executed speedily, therefore the heart of the sons of men is fully set in them to do evil."

There is a recurring statement found in the book of Judges that reinforces this truth. Judges 17:6 says: "In those days there was no king in Israel, but every man did that which was right in his own eyes."

Habakkuk is to be commended for his concern over the spiritual conditions that prevailed in Judah. He is expressing that concern to God. The negative aspect of his expression is that he charges God of being delinquent or negligent in responding.

Based upon the review and recommendation of another person, I recently purchased a book. The book deals with various things that cause *gaps* in our relationship with God. One story related, as an illustration, how a new church had been started, but in a short while there was a felt need to discontinue meeting. In the struggle to decide what to do, the lead pastor and wife went hiking. They found a suitable place and stopped to pray. The prayers were very intense and earnest. After the prayer time, they lay on their backs looking upward at a tree. Then they added an addendum to the prayers. It went like this: "God, if you have heard these prayers, let one, and only one, leaf fall from the tree." As they lay waiting and watching, one lone leaf came floating downward. This they interpreted as a sign that God had heard their prayers and by this sign gave confirmation and approval of the course of action they had formulated relating to the church.

It appears that this couple attached greater significance to a falling leaf than to the promises of God. In this instance a falling leaf is seen as a superior revelation to all the promises of God that are recorded in his word, telling us that he will always hear and answer the prayers of his people. Both this modern-day couple and Habakkuk really needed to know and understand that God always hears the prayer of any one of his people. There is never a need for further confirmation of that fact other than the promises contained within the pages of the Bible. Just pray and believe and know that God is listening and responding.

Now back to the subject of this chapter of our study. The chapter opens the door to a significant question in relation to answered prayer. How could Habakkuk know if God had indeed answered his prayer? If he could know, what was God's answer? And when did God answer? Or exactly what was God intending to teach Habakkuk about prayer?

PRECEPT # 8
Prayer will result in identifying God's activity.

Several factors will characterize God's answer, and these will convince Habakkuk that God has answered.

1. God's work is eternally marvelous.

    Behold you among the heathen, and regard, and wonder marvelously.

2. God's work is eternally contemporary.

    I will work a work in your days

3. God's work is eternally incomprensible.

    I will work a work in your days, which you will not believe, though it be told you.

God's response to Habakkuk's indictment awakened in Habakkuk a confession of God's greatness and an understanding of His planned purposes for Babylon.

1. God had chosen to use Babylon as a tool of judgment.

   O LORD, you have ordained them for judgment; (Habakkuk 1:12)

2. God was using Babylon as an instrument for correction.

   O mighty God, thou hast established them for correction. (Habakkuk 1:12)

Chapter Six

Are You Not?

Habakkuk 1:12-17

Are you not from everlasting, O LORD my God,
mine Holy One? we shall not die. O LORD, you
have ordained them for judgment; and, O mighty
God, you have established them for correction. You
are of purer eyes than to behold evil, and cannot
look on iniquity: wherefore look you upon them
that deal treacherously, and hold your tongue
when the wicked devours the man that is more
righteous than he? And make men as the fishes of
the sea, as the creeping things, that have no ruler
over them? They take up all of them with the angle,
they catch them in their net, and gather them in
their drag: therefore, they rejoice and are glad.
Therefore, they sacrifice unto their net and burn
incense unto their drag; because by them their por-
tion is fat, and their meat plenteous. Shall they
therefore empty their net, and not spare continu-
ally to slay the nations?

I read with much interest and blessing that which such persons as A. W. Tozer have written about the character of God. It remains a mystery as to how so many of we Christians fail to study and grasp God's real nature–His love, His mercy, His holiness, His presence, His power, His glory and majesty, His sovereignty, and a host of other great attributes that characterize our great and glorious God. Tozer writes in his book *The Pursuit of God*:

> *The modern scientist has lost God amid the wonders of His world; we Christians are in real danger of losing God amid the wonders of His Word. We have almost forgotten that God is a person and, as such, can be cultivated as any person can. It is inherent in personality to be able to know other personalities, but full knowledge of one personality by another cannot be achieved in one encounter. It is only after long and loving mental intercourse that the full possibilities of both can be explored.*

J. I. Packer leads us to meditate on the greatness and majesty of God when he writes:

"To whom then will you liken me, or shall I be equal? says the Holy One." (Isaiah 40:25).

> *This question rebukes wrong thoughts about God. "Your thoughts of God are too human," said Luther to Erasmus. This is where most of us go astray. Our thoughts of God are not great enough; we fail to reckon with the reality of his limitless wisdom and power. Because we ourselves are limited and weak, we imagine that at some point God is too, and find it hard to believe that he is not. We think of God as too much like we are. Put this mistake right,*

*says God; learn to acknowledge the full majesty of
your incomparable God and Savior.*[1]

PRECEPT # 9
Prayer will develop a more intimate fellowship with God.

Our progress in the study of Habakkuk brings us to learn of his
God (Habakkuk 1:12–17). Habakkuk has engaged himself in a
conversation with God that shows clearly that his acquaintance
with God has much room for improvement and needs some attention. He shows himself as being in need of developing a more
intimate acquaintance and greater comprehension of the God with
whom he is speaking. That last sentence describes a category of
believers who are inclined to accuse God of failure to answer a
prayer. We would never accuse God of not hearing a prayer if we
were more intimately acquainted with Him and knew His heart.
Nor would we fall into the trap of thinking that God had failed to
answer a prayer if we were better informed about the character
of God and had found Him faithful and true in all his promises.
Therefore, we along with Habakkuk need to cultivate our relationship with our wonderful Lord and our Savior, Jesus Christ. Peter
admonishes us to do so when he writes:

> *But grow in grace, and in the knowledge of our
> Lord and Savior Jesus Christ. To him be glory both
> now and forever. Amen.* (2 Peter 3:18)

Prayer is, by the simplest definition, a conversation with God.
Conversation is one avenue of communion that allows one personality to gain knowledge and understanding of another kindred

---

[1]   KNOWING GOD, J. I. Packer, IVP Books, 20th Anniversary ed. Edition,
     September 26, 2011; p. 88

personality. In this section of Habakkuk, chapter 1, we are allowed to enter into this developing relationship between Habakkuk and his God. As such we must acknowledge that we are on very holy ground. And we must conduct ourselves appropriately and maintain an attitude of the highest reverence.

Recently I have been drawn to meditate on and study Colossians 4:2:

continue in prayer and watch in the same with thanksgiving

and 1 Thessalonians 5:17:

pray without ceasing

In the Colossians verse, the word *continue* means "to follow a consistent and regular pattern or to be steadfast." It means to be strong and unremitting in prayer. In the 1 Thessalonians verse, the words *without ceasing* mean to pray frequently and spontaneously. I have come to realize that my praying has for the most part been *circumstance oriented* when it should have been *fellowship oriented*. By *circumstance oriented* I mean I have been drawn to pray when some issue arises that I do not think I can handle alone. By *fellowship oriented* I mean I should have been praying frequently and spontaneously and having fellowship with Jesus Christ in a regular and unremitting pattern of prayer. My prayers should take the form of *a dialogue* and not the form of a *monologue*. It seems that *circumstance oriented* prayer takes the form of a *monologue* while *fellowship oriented* prayer seems to take the form of a *dialogue*. In *circumstance oriented* prayer I am too much occupied telling God about my problems and felt needs to hear much of anything he might say to me, so my prayer becomes a *monologue*. When I pray like that, I monopolize the conversation and I do not allow God to enter into the conversation and speak to me. In *fellowship oriented* prayer, God and I talk with each other and the prayer becomes a *dialogue*, and that which would otherwise seem to be a crisis and/or traumatic event becomes a more nearly normal issue in my fellowship with my Lord Jesus. This old gospel song (which we seldom sing anymore) illustrates these thoughts:

> I come to the garden alone, *(for fellowship)*
> While the dew is still on the roses, *(consistent, regular prayer)*
> And the voice I hear falling on my ear *(dialogue)*
> The Son of God discloses. *(the voice reveals the presence of Jesus)*
> And He walks with me, and He talks with me, *(fellowship and dialogue)*
> And He tells me I am His own; *(fellowship)*
> And the joy we share as we tarry there (*joy unspeakable and full of glory*)
> None other has ever known. (*These things have I spoken unto you, that my joy might remain in you, and that your joy might be full. John 15:11*)

The application I make is for all who read this to establish prayer as a *dialogue* with God (*Pray without ceasing*) rather than a *monologue* to God. When something arises that is perceived to be a crisis, one can have *fellowship* with God, which allows a *dialogue* with Him to evolve. In the *dialogue* God can make known to a person His view of the situation, and He just may tell *why*. In either instance the person will better understand God and love Him more. Also, God will be glorified, and the person will be edified by the conversation *(fellowship)*. In this way the person can be strong in prayer:

> *Continue in prayer and watch in the same with thanksgiving* (Colossians 4:2).

Habakkuk appears to be having problems with his prayers because he was speaking in a monologue to God:

> *O LORD, how long shall I cry, and thou wilt not hear! even cry out unto thee of violence, and thou wilt not save!* (Habakkuk 1:2).

In his prayer he asks some rhetorical questions about God. Lest we have forgotten, a rhetorical question simply does not require an answer. Implied in the question is the answer. There is a total of four questions included in his statement about God's character (Habakkuk 1:12-13). They are:

(1) *"O LORD my God, my Holy One; Are you not from everlasting?"*

The question: *"Are you not from everlasting?"*

The answer: YES, God is eternal.

(2) *"O LORD, have you not ordained them for judgment?"*

The question: *"Have you not ordained them for judgment?"*

The answer: Yes. God has ordained the Chaldeans to be his instruments of judgment.

(3) *"O mighty God, have you not established them for correction?"*

The question: *"Have you not established them for correcting Judah?"*

The answer: Yes. God has established the Chaldeans to be his means of correcting Judah.

(4) *"are you not of purer eyes than to behold evil and cannot look upon iniquity?"*

The question: *"Are your eyes too pure to look upon evil"?*

The answer: Yes. God's eyes are too pure to look upon sin?"

These questions paint for us the beautiful picture of the character of God. But Habakkuk has concluded in his mind that God is not acting within the framework of that character. Because of this faulty conclusion, Habakkuk brings his indictment against God as not answering his prayer.

The portrait of God that Habakkuk holds is, as mentioned before, to be considered as a beautiful and perhaps correct picture. It is a picture that each of us needs to see in HD (high definition) colors when we are having a prayer conversation with God. The conversation will be greatly improved and become more meaningful if we can in some fashion visualize the one with whom we are speaking. Having in mind such an image could hold potential for enhancement of our prayers.

(1.) God is eternal:

Are you not from everlasting, O LORD my God, my Holy One?

Habakkuk is not so much asking a question as he is making a statement of fact. The sentence is as much a declaration as an interrogation. He is making a declaration that expects, if not requires, an affirmative reply. In the immediately preceding verse, it is revealed that Babylon has been "imputing his power unto his god." The prophet and Babylon are placed in sharp contrast. Babylon's strength is the nation's god. Habakkuk places his confidence in the living, eternal God. Notice the word *LORD* is in all capital letters, indicating that Yahweh or Jehovah is Habakkuk's God.

The English translation of the name is "O LORD my God." Hebrew is יְהוָה אֱלֹהַי or "Jehovah Elohim."[2] Here we have one of the dual names for God, the use of which began as early as the Genesis account of creation. In the Genesis account of creation, Jehovah-Elohim personally shaped and fashioned man's physical body. In the account of creation given in Genesis, God is said to be directly involved forty-six times. It is intended that we understand clearly that the human body is especially the direct product of the creative activity of Jehovah-Elohim. Habakkuk's God is Habakkuk's creator, as well as the creator of heaven and earth.

(2)   God is Holy–(*qadosh*-קְדוֹשׁי):

In the Old Testament *qadosh* has a strong religious connotation. In one sense the word describes an object or place or period of time as "holy" with the meaning of "devoted" or "dedicated" to a particular purpose. Scripture references using this word (*qadosh*–קְדשִׁי) show its use in its application to various matters. The garments of the Aaronic priests were *holy*. Thus, there are holy things (Exodus 31:10). The sabbath day was *holy*. So here we have *holy*

---

[2] See discussion of this name in my book *His Excellent Name*; p. 40; copyright Xulon Press 2009

time (Exodus 31:14). The ground where Moses stood was *holy*. Here we have a *holy place* (Exodus 3:5. The people themselves were to be *holy*. Therefore, we have *holy people* (Leviticus 20:7, 26). In such uses as these we are given an understanding of the general, yet special, use of the word (*qadosh*–קָדֹשׁ). In other scripture references the word carries the commonly recognized concept of separation. The Bible leads us to believe that all holiness is derived from a relationship to God. Only God is holy (1 Peter 1:16). Holiness is attributed to any person or thing because that person or thing has a specific relationship to God. The description we have been given of the society around Habakkuk is clearly that of unholiness. That is their characteristic because of their rejection of God.

(3)   God is just.

In the last two lines of v. 12, Habakkuk is seen as understanding God to be active in bringing about judgment and justice. The nation of Babylon is to be used by God to do this. Habakkuk's statement is:

> *O LORD, you have ordained them for judgment;*
> *and, O mighty God, you have established them for*
> *correction.*

Even while making such a significant confession, Habakkuk does not comprehend its relevance to the truth of this verse. We must come to know that *judgment* (מִשְׁפָּט–*mishpat*) is the act of sitting as a judge, hearing a case, and rendering a proper verdict, which is here referred to as *correction* (יָכַח–yakach). In most uses of this word it is evident that there is a value judgment involved.

(4)   God is pure–(*tahor*–טָהוֹר)

*You are of purer eyes than to behold evil and cannot
look on iniquity.*

The word for *purer* means "clean; pure." The word denotes the
absence of impurity, filthiness, defilement, or imperfection. It is
applied in reference to substances that are genuine or unadulter-
ated as well as describing an unstained condition of a spiritual or
ceremonial nature.

Gold is a material frequently said to be free of baser ingredients.
Therefore, much of the tabernacle and temple was made of or covered with gold to symbolize the purity of the instruments and the
building, and even of God himself. This was indicative of the fact
that God, to whom these things were dedicated, is holy.

I have confidence in describing Habakkuk's statement about God's
character as being a little facetious. What he said is definitely a
correct description of God. But it appears quite clearly that the
intent behind the statement is to charge God with acting out of
character in the way he is relating to Habakkuk and his prayer
for Judah. He is accusing God of presenting himself as holy, pure,
just, and eternal. But God is behaving as if he is of an opposite
character.

Not long ago I read an essay written by C. S. Lewis in which he
argued against a person so far removed in time from the writers of
the Bible, as we are, trying to impute to those writers any mind-set
or purpose for that which they wrote. And no claim is here made
for exemption from doing so. But in reading this section of
Habakkuk, he is heard talking with God about God's failure to

listen and respond to his prayer. He also charges God with making him look upon violence and iniquity while God Himself claims to be absolutely pure and holy. He then indicts God by attributing to Him the responsibility of creating the very evil people of Babylon while using them to judge Judah. It all seems to be so contradictory to Habakkuk. Such a charge against Habakkuk is based, at least in part, upon 1:13. Think about what is being said in that verse:

> *You are of purer eyes than to behold evil, and cannot look on iniquity: wherefore look you upon them that deal treacherously, and hold your tongue when the wicked devours the man that is more righteous than he?*

Again, Habakkuk is saying that God is too pure to even look on evil and is of such holy character that he cannot look upon iniquity, yet God watches Babylon deal treacherously with other nations and Habakkuk says that God does nothing while the righteous are devoured by the wicked. Habakkuk sees God as not acting like God.

At this point God intrudes Himself into the conversation. Habakkuk has made some very serious charges about God's response to his prayers. The remarks actually impeach the character of God. The error in Habakkuk's statements must be given a responsive correction. In His response, God gives Habakkuk a very challenging assignment:

> *Behold you among the heathen, and regard, and wonder marvelously: for I will work a work in your days, which you will not believe, though it be told you.*

The statement of God merits a more thorough and detailed study.

1.   God's response is universal (v.5).

> *Behold you among the heathen, and regard, and wonder marvelously: for I will work a work in your days, which you will not believe, though it be told you.*

Behold–(רָאָה–ra' ah)–"To see, observe, perceive, get acquainted with, gain understanding, examine, look after (see to), choose, discover." Basically *ra›ah* connotes seeing with one's eyes, but it can also mean *"to observe"* (Judges 16:27). Another possible meaning is "to perceive," "to ascertain," or "to be consciously aware of" (Deuteronomy 4:28). A fourth idea of seeing is "to examine" (Genesis 11:5).

2.   God's response is prophetic (v. 6-11)

> *Behold you among the heathen, and regard, and wonder marvelously.*

*"wonder marvelously"–(tamah–*וְהִתַּמְּהוּ *)–*means to be astounded, be stunned, be amazed, be dumbfounded.

"behold... regard"- same words used in 1:3 for "show" and "behold."

In Habakkuk 1:4 he complained that God caused him to look upon "iniquity" and placed before him "strife and contention." His words are:

Why do you show me iniquity and cause me to behold grievance? for spoiling and violence are before me: and there are that raise up strife and contention. Therefore, the law is slacked, and judgment does never go forth: for the wicked does compass about the righteous; therefore, wrong judgment proceeds.

But now in 1:13 he accuses God of looking upon wrong actions and remaining speechless while the wicked perpetrate wrong on the righteous.

You are of purer eyes than to behold evil, and cannot look on iniquity: wherefore look you upon them that deal treacherously, and hold your tongue when the wicked devours the man that is more righteous than he?

In summary Habakkuk has in his mind the understanding that:

(1.) God overlooks sin and simply ignores it.

(2.) But he also has a mental picture of a God who will not tolerate sin. He will act in judgment.

(3.) To confuse the matter still more he accuses God of refusing to take action against sin—*he holds his tongue*

Habakkuk seems to see in God a contradiction he deplores. He speaks to God, saying:

And make men as the fishes of the sea, as the creeping things, that have no ruler over them? They take up all of them with the angle, they catch

*them in their net, and gather them in their drag:
therefore, they rejoice and are glad. Therefore,
they sacrifice unto their net, and burn incense
unto their drag; because by them their portion is
fat, and their meat plenteous. Shall they therefore
empty their net, and not spare continually to slay
the nations?*

Review the flow of the conversation between Habakkuk and God.

Habakkuk (vs. 2-4):

*"You are not listening. You are making me look
upon sin and wrong doing."*

*O LORD, how long shall I cry, and you will not
hear! even cry out unto you of violence, and you
will not save! Why do you show me iniquity and
cause me to behold grievance? for spoiling and
violence are before me: and there are that raise
up strife and contention. Therefore, the law is
slacked, and judgment does never go forth: for the
wicked does compass about the righteous; therefore, wrong judgment proceeds.*

God (Habakkuk 5-11) instructs Habakkuk to look around, to look
throughout the world, and you will discover that I am doing a work
at which you will *wonder marvelously.* I have, and I am answering
your prayer. You are just not looking, or you do not recognize what
you are seeing.

Behold you among the heathen, and regard, and wonder marvelously: for I will work a work in your days, which you will not believe, though it be told you. For, lo, I raise up the Chaldeans, that bitter and hasty nation, which shall march through the breadth of the land, to possess the dwelling-places that are not theirs. They are terrible and dreadful: their judgment and their dignity shall proceed of themselves. Their horses also are swifter than the leopards and are more fierce than the evening wolves: and their horsemen shall spread themselves, and their horsemen shall come from far; they shall fly as the eagle that hastens to eat. They shall come all for violence: their faces shall sup up as the east wind, and they shall gather the captivity as the sand. And they shall scoff at the kings, and the princes shall be a scorn unto them: they shall deride every strong hold; for they shall heap dust and take it. Then shall his mind change, and he shall pass over, and offend, imputing this his power unto his god.

Habakkuk (1:14-17):

And make men as the fishes of the sea, as the creeping things, that have no ruler over them? They take up all of them with the angle, they catch them in their net, and gather them in their drag: therefore, they rejoice and are glad. Therefore, they sacrifice unto their net, and burn incense unto their drag; because by them their portion is fat, and their meat plenteous. Shall they therefore

empty their net, and not spare continually to slay
the nations?

In this paragraph the activity of fishing is the metaphor of choice to help illustrate the process Babylon is using to get control of the nations around her. The words *angle, net,* and *drag,* refer to something like a fishhook, something perforated like a net, and something to drag around like a net. All of these are tools of fishing and they fit into the illustration being used here of Babylon's getting rich by fishing.

And make men as the fishes of the sea, as the creeping
things, that have no ruler over them. (v. 14)

God is the creator of men. The word used here for *men* is אָדָם–
'adam. It can have several applicable meanings. It can refer to persons simply as *human* (that is, a single human being of either sex). It can also refer to humankind, a class of being created by God with a focus as a class distinct from animals, plants, or even spiritual beings. The word is gender neutral. The creature (אָדָם–
'adam) is seen as being weak and defenseless. Babylon, under the metaphor of fishes and creeping things, ignores or denies that God is ruler; therefore, she has no restraints on what she can do.

They take up all of them with the angle, they catch
them in their net, and gather them in their drag:
therefore, they rejoice and are glad. (v. 15)

They is a pronoun referring to Babylon. Nations are being captured like fish caught by a net. The catch is great, and the fishermen rejoice. This verse pictures Babylon as very calloused and indifferent to the plight of conquered nations.

*Therefore, they sacrifice unto their net and burn
incense unto their drag; because by them their portion is fat, and their meat plenteous.* (v. 16)

The net becomes an idol because of Babylon becoming rich
through the conquest of others.

*Shall they therefore empty their net, and not spare
continually to slay the nations?* (v. 17)

Babylon casually empties the net (the latest nation conquered)
and moves on to another conquest. Habakkuk is thus heard to be
saying: "I know you are a great God—eternal, holy, just, and pure.
I know that you cannot look upon sin. But IF this is your character, why do you allow men as fishes to be caught in a net and
used to make the fishermen fat? When they have caught and prof-
ited from the fish they have caught, they worship the nets used to
catch the fish. All the while you allow them to continuously slay
other nations."

Habakkuk reveals to us the enigma that he holds in his mind. He
feels that God is eternal, holy, just, and pure, but he cannot recon-
cile what is happening to the nation of Judah with this concept of
God. It appears as if Habakkuk is asking: "Why does God allow
such to happen? Why does God not hear my prayer? I call out to
him, but he does not answer. Why?"

Such a quandary is not unique to Habakkuk. History is filled with
stories of persons of kindred mind who have queried God in like
manner. One of those may well be you or me.

A summary of what we have just read in Habakkuk will help get a much clearer picture of what is transpiring. Habakkuk feels that God is not listening or responding to his cry and prayer. God responds to his complaint by directing his attention to the bigger picture of world events. Habakkuk then issues a statement of his concept of God's character. That statement needs to be considered with an intense effort to get a mental picture of what Habakkuk is feeling as well as the reason behind what he says about God. We can do this by carefully studying the verses that follow (Habakkuk 1:14–17). In these verses Habakkuk appears to be saying that although God is eternal, holy, pure, and just, He is not acting in accordance with his character. He has made men and left them defenseless. The use of the word *men* is a metaphor for the nations being overrun by Babylon, especially Judah. They are conquered ("They take up all of them with the angle, they catch them in their net, and gather them in their drag: therefore, they rejoice and are glad") and are used for profit by their captors. The captors (Babylon) then rejoice in their conquest and profit and continue their efforts at world conquest (v.17).

Habakkuk's statement of facts is correct. But in making the statement of 1:12-17, he is impeaching God by accusing God of not acting in accordance with His character. He is making an accusatory statement against God. He yields to what seems to be an ongoing temptation to all Believers and blames God for what is happening. Now, God is sovereign, as stated earlier. But it appears that what we have in Habakkuk is a statement indicting God and charging Him with guilt by not acting appropriately in the defense of his people.

Again, Habakkuk seems to subscribe to the popular concept that God's people are to be exempt from trouble, problems, disease, and suffering. If such calamities come upon them, they can merely tell God to remove them, and God will do so immediately according to their request and timing. Such a flawed premise ultimately leads to a false conclusion. Romans 8:28 needs to be brought to bear in such a situation as the one faced by Habakkuk.

> *And we know that all things work together for good to them that love God, to them who are the called according to his purpose.*

Another possible reading for this verse in Romans 8 is:

> *And we know that God is at work in everything for the good of those who love God and are called according to his purpose for them.* (Rom. 8:28 NLT2)

Habakkuk seemed unable to see this truth and so he complained about what God was allowing to happen and about God's seeming inactivity and lack of response to his prayers.

Chapter Seven

Watch To See

Habakkuk 2: 1-20

I will stand upon my watch, and set me upon the tower, and will watch to see what he will say unto me, and what I shall answer when I am reproved. And the LORD answered me, and said, Write the vision, and make it plain upon tables, that he may run that reads it. For the vision is yet for an appointed time, but at the end it shall speak, and not lie: though it tarry, wait for it; because it will surely come, it will not tarry. Behold, his soul which is lifted up is not upright in him: but the just shall live by his faith.

Yes also, because he transgresses by wine, he is a proud man, neither keeps at home, who enlarges his desire as hell, and is as death, and cannot be satisfied, but gathers unto him all nations, and heaps unto him all people: Shall not all these take up a parable against him, and a taunting proverb against him, and say, Woe to him that increases that which is not his! how long? and to him that loads himself with thick clay! Shall they not rise up suddenly that shall bite you, and awake that shall vex you, and you shall be for booties unto them? Because you have spoiled many nations, all the remnant of the people shall spoil you; because of men's blood, and for the violence of the land, of the city, and of all that dwell therein. Woe to him that covets an evil covetousness to his house, that he may set his nest on high, that he may be delivered from the power of evil! You have consulted shame to your house by cutting off many people and have sinned against your soul. For the stone shall cry out of the wall, and the beam out of the timber shall answer it. Woe to him that builds a town with blood and establishes a city by iniquity! Behold, is it not of the LORD of hosts that the people shall labor in the very fire, and the people shall weary themselves for very vanity? For the earth shall be filled with the knowledge of the glory of the LORD, as the waters cover the sea.

Woe unto him that gives his neighbor drink, that puts your bottle to him, and make him drunk also, that you may look on their nakedness! You are filled with shame for glory: drink you also, and let your uncircumcision be revealed: the cup of the LORD'S right hand shall be turned unto you, and shameful spewing shall be on your glory. For the violence of Lebanon shall cover you, and the spoil of beasts, which made them afraid, because of men's blood, and for the violence of the land, of the city, and of all that dwell therein. What profits the graven image that the maker thereof has graven it; the molten image, and a teacher of lies, that the maker of his work trusts therein, to make dumb idols? Woe unto him that says to the wood, Awake; to the dumb stone, Arise, it shall teach! Behold, it is laid over with gold and silver, and there is no breath at all in the middle of it. But the LORD is in his holy temple: let all the earth keep silence before him.

In Habakkuk chapter 1, we heard Habakkuk complain about what he thought was God's failure to hear and answer his prayer. The prophet now realizes that he has falsely charged God. He is now resolved to take position on a guard tower from which he will obtain an unobstructed view of contemporary events. This decision on the part of Habakkuk seems to be largely prompted by the instruction of God given to him in 1:5. That verse records God's instruction for Habakkuk to look around in the non-Jewish world of his day and discover just what God is doing. When Habakkuk obeys God's instruction, he will be caused to *wonder marvelously* by what he discovers. He had cried out to God for help as he watched his homeland drift away from God and place herself in a position to be judged by God. But God "caused" him to see so much godless activity that he felt abandoned.

Habakkuk complained about God's inactivity. God gave him an answer that distressed him even more. God says He is going to send the wicked nation of Babylon as an instrument of judgment. This is not the answer for which Habakkuk was expecting. In fact, he finds it hard to believe that God would use a nation more sinful and evil than Judah to establish His righteousness. For Habakkuk, this seems inconsistent. It doesn't make sense. But he doesn't give up on God.

God instructs Habakkuk to look around among the nations of his world and see that God is doing a marvelous and wonderful work.

> *Behold, among the heathen, and regard, and wonder marvelously: for I will work a work in your days, which you will not believe, though it be told you* (Habakkuk 1:5).

Habakkuk completes his complaint against God and hears God's initial response and instructions. He now knows that his perception that God is being delinquent in hearing and answering prayer is wrong and deserves a strong rebuke and reprimand. He decides that he will find a vantage point and just watch and see what God does. He says:

> *I will stand upon my watch, and set me upon the tower, and will watch to see what he will say unto me, and what I shall answer when I am reproved.* (Habakkuk 2:1)

This verse describes Habakkuk's obedient response to God's instructions given in 1:5, in which God said to Habakkuk:

> *Behold, among the heathen, and regard, and wonder marvelously: for I will work a work in your days, which you will not believe, though it be told you.*

PRECEPT #10
To classify prayer as unanswered is an indictment of God.

The first thing to be learned about Habakkuk in chapter 2. is his resolve:

> *I will stand upon my watch, and set me upon the*
> *tower, and will watch to see what he will say unto*
> *me, and what I shall answer when I am reproved.*

The verb *will* is used, or implied, several times in 2:1. It expresses Habakkuk's planned response to God:

1. *I will set me upon my tower* (paraphrase).

I will locate a vantage point from which I can watch with an unobstructed view and climb upon it.

2. *I will stand upon my watch.*

I will stand awake, alert and at attention.

3. *I will watch to see.*

I will seek to discover that which God is actually doing. Please note that the verse reads "watch to see." The particle "to" is significant in use here giving the idea of intent or purpose.

4. I will listen (implied) to what God will say to me.

I will become humble, teachable, and obedient.

5. *What I will answer what I shall say when I am reproved.*

The ultimate goal of the decision is presented as being the appropriate response to God's rebuke, which will surely be experienced by the prophet.

Read on in the saga of Habakkuk's conversation with God and discover the wonderful outcome. Habakkuk learned when his prayer was answered. He had been telling God when to answer and what to do in answer to his prayer. Therefore, he did not recognize God's answer. He had thought the answer would come in the time and manner he had described to God. It would appear at the time and method he had designated in his praying. Isaiah gives us information about how God times His answers.

> *And it shall come to pass, that before they call, I will answer; and while they are yet speaking, I will hear."* (Isaiah 65:24)

Daniel gives us an example of God answering prayer is this fashion.

> *Then said he unto me, Fear not, Daniel: for from the first day that thou didst set thine heart to understand, and to chasten thyself before thy God, thy words were heard, and I am come for thy words.* (Daniel 10:12)

Jeremiah reports on the word he heard from God:

> *Moreover the word of the LORD came unto Jeremiah the second time, while he was yet shut up in the court of the prison, saying, ² Thus saith*

*the LORD the maker thereof, the LORD that
formed it, to establish it; the LORD is his name;
³ Call unto me, and I will answer you, and show
you great and mighty things, which you know not.*
(Jeremiah 33:1-3)

*And it shall come to pass, that before they call, I will answer; and
while they are yet speaking, I will hear.* (Isaiah 65:24)

Jeremiah tells us about the truth God taught him in this regard:

*Moreover the word of the LORD came unto
Jeremiah the second time, while he was yet shut
up in the court of the prison, saying, Thus saith
the LORD the maker thereof, the LORD that
formed it, to establish it; the LORD is his name;
Call unto me, and I will answer you, and show
you great and mighty things, which you know not.*
(Jeremiah 33:1- 3)

The most likely reason for the failure to discern the answer is
because the prayer was in the form of telling God what to do
and when to act. It appears that many may fail to recognize an
answered prayer because they fail to recognize the nature of the
answer. The failure to recognize the answer is because the prayer
request was nothing other than instructing God in what to do. If we
tell God what to do, we will likely be unable to discern the form
in which the answer comes. The lack of recognition of the answer
will be because it is not in the form and manner prescribed by us
in making the request. Habakkuk's prayer was an attempt to tell
God about Judah's conditions. He seems to be expecting God to
answer his prayer by altering the contemporary conditions in the

nation. We learned from Habakkuk's complaint in chapter 1 that nothing was changed in Judah; therefore, he assumed that God had neither heard nor answered. But God told Habakkuk to "behold" (look throughout the surrounding nations) what He was doing in the non-Jewish nations around him, particularly in Babylon.

The word *stand* (*amad*-אָעֱמֹדָה) means "to take one's stand; stand here or be there; stand still." The basic meaning of this verb is "to stand upright." It is what a soldier does while on guard duty (2 Samuel 18:30). From this basic meaning comes the meaning "to be established, immovable, and standing upright" on a single spot.

The phrase "stand upon my watch" (מִשְׁמֶרֶת—*mishmereth*) is a military term. The NASB translates the word as "guard-post." It involves entrusting a trained individual with the responsibility of looking for potential threats to the community of which he is a part. The faithful watchman denies himself normal hours of sleep so that he might be awake while others sleep. He does not go without sleep but takes his sleep at another time so that he might watch. He trains his eyes and does the right thing when he sees a threat. Staying at his post requires commitment!

The word *tower* means "a bulwark." It is a protected, enclosed area, usually on the wall of a city, from where a watchman could obtain a distant, unobstructed view and detect any enemy activity–or the approach of a messenger. Sometimes the rampart was around a vineyard to provide a deterrent to thieves.

It is likely that the words *watch* (*mišmeret* or observation station) and the *tower* ("*māṣôr*", watchtower or fortress) was used metaphorically in reference to the prophet's attitude-a resolve to carefully and objectively observe contemporary events-rather than his physical location. Habakkuk decides to take the character and position of a watchman that looks carefully at the surrounding scene. He will take a position on the ramparts, the high places, to get a better perspective.

Habakkuk describes his resolve with the phrase "and will watch to see" (וְאֲחַיְצָבָה) (צָפָה–*tsaphah*) (watch). The statement means "to overlay, spy, keep watch." Perhaps in most uses, the connotation of "to spy" would be the most widely used meaning. In this instance, however, the idea of keeping watch seems more accurate. It expresses the thought of a continual watch while waiting to determine what God is really doing.

Habakkuk refers in 2:1 to being "reproved" (*towkechah*-תּוֹכַחְתִּי). The idea in this verb is that of a rebuke, correction, reproof, punishment, chastisement. Some see in this word the idea of "argument" in the sense of one person trying to prove another wrong. The idea is not so much that of controversy as is that of a difference of opinion. God is challenging, will challenge, and has challenged Habakkuk's conclusion concerning the role he should have in responding to Habakkuk's prayer.

Isaiah 62:1-7 has an interesting reference to the "watchtowers" that may shed some light on this verse in Habakkuk. Isaiah writes:

> *For Zion's sake will I not hold my peace, and for Jerusalem's sake I will not rest, until the righteousness thereof goes forth as brightness, and the salvation thereof as a lamp that burns. And the Gentiles shall see your righteousness, and all kings your glory: and you shall be called by a new name, which the mouth of the LORD shall name.*

107

You shall also be a crown of glory in the hand of the LORD, and a royal diadem in the hand of your God. You shall no more be termed Forsaken; neither shall your land any more be termed Desolate: but you shall be called Hephzibah, and your land Beulah: for the LORD delights in you, and your land shall be married. For as a young man marries a virgin, so shall your sons marry you: and as the bridegroom rejoices over the bride, so shall your God rejoice over you. I have set watchmen upon your walls, O Jerusalem, which shall never hold their peace day nor night: you that make mention of the LORD, keep not silence, And, give him no rest until he establishes and until he makes Jerusalem a praise in the earth.

Isaiah's prophecy predates Habakkuk by several hundred years, but it seems to be a prelude to God's promised answer to Habakkuk's prayer. The metaphorical use of the "watchtowers" by both Isaiah and Habakkuk highlight the importance of their use in God's answer. Isaiah pictures the towers as being occupied by watchmen who appear to have taken their position in order to observe contemporary activity and to be better able to pray for God's involvement. Habakkuk's position was taken in order to better observe God's involvement in response to his prayer. The relationship these two passages have to each other is that of earnest prayer being made to God for his intervention in the affairs of the nation and of watching to see just how God answers and saves the nation.

At this point Habakkuk is reserving any more comment until he understands current events better. He knows that God is about to "reprove" him. His words are "when I am reproved." He does not say "if." He now knows that he has impeached the character of God when he accused God of not listening and of not taking action. He knows that God always listens to and answers the cry of his people. But he thought God was not listening to his call. He also was convinced that God always acted in response to the cry of his people. But from his burdened position, it appeared to him that God was not paying attention to current prayer. God's inactivity was confusing. Habakkuk no doubt thought his request to be legitimate and consistent with the character and will of God. But God's proposed activity is even more confusing. God showed Habakkuk that He was in the process of using Babylon (the Chaldeans) to bring His judgment upon Judah. So, Habakkuk, through conversation with God, has come to the conclusion that not all workings of God can be understood by our own reasoning. He therefore plans to find a place from which he can observe and verify what God is currently doing, in part in response to his prayer and in part simply working to accomplish his overall plan in the world over which he remains forever sovereign.

After Habakkuk has been engaged in a conversation with God (1:2-17) he knows that God will rebuke (correct) him for his practice and perception of prayer. There are several problems discovered in Habakkuk's concept and practice of prayer:

1. The pattern of his praying presents the first problem. He is apparently telling God what to do rather than asking God to do something,

> *O LORD, how long shall I cry, and you will not hear! even cry out unto you of violence, and you will not save! Why do you show me iniquity and*

> *cause me to behold grievance? for spoiling and*
> *violence are before me: and there are that raise up*
> *strife and contention.*

Habakkuk reminded God that he had called the sins of Judah to His attention and told God about violence, iniquity, and spoiling, etc.

Now, here it seems is a common occurrence among contemporary believers. We pray for a person who has a catastrophic illness, which is well and good. But the prayer tends to be nothing more than instructing God to heal and when to do the healing. We, it seems, are prone to tell God to heal rather than ask that our Lord Jesus, the Great Physician, be glorified through the illness. According to Biblical teaching, the illness may have a special purpose in God's management of our lives. Suffering *does* have a positive purpose and place in God's plans. The television program announced with bold letters all across the screen: "God wants you well." There may perhaps be some truth in that statement depending on how it is interpreted. But God's word declares that there was "a messenger of Satan" given to Paul for whose departure he prayed. He was given grace to bear rather than the removal of the thorn. When we pray for such a person to be healed, we just might, however unwittingly, be telling God to abort His plans and yield to our desires rather than work in the circumstances to bring glory and honor to His name (Romans 8:28). The outcome is that when healing does, or does not, come, God is not glorified, and we are not satisfied. Psalm 50:15 says this: "And call upon me in the day of trouble: I will deliver thee, and thou shalt glorify me."

I suggest that we learn to pray for God *to minister* to those who have an illness, or some other major problem, without instructing Him in *how to minister*. By instructing God we may in effect be asking Him to abort His plans. That would be making the individual equal to, or even superior to, God. Think about the following interpretation of Romans 8:28:

> *And we know that God is working in all things for good to them that love Him, to them who are the called according to his purpose.*

2. The response of God to the prayer of Habakkuk presents another problem. Conditions seemed to indicate that if God had indeed answered Habakkuk's prayer Judah would be experiencing none of the listed conditions:

> *Why dost thou shew me iniquity, and cause me to behold grievance? for spoiling and violence are before me: and there are that raise up strife and contention. Therefore the law is slacked, and judgment doth never go forth: for the wicked doth compass about the righteous; therefore wrong judgment proceedeth.*

All items in this list are things Habakkuk accused God of not addressing in his prayer.

The word *reprove* means "to be corrected." He charged God with being derelict in His duty. God will "correct" him and that he knows right well and confesses such both to himself and to God. He is challenged to really observe God at work.

> *Behold you among the heathen, and regard, and wonder marvelously: for I will work a work in your days, which you will not believe, though it be told*

*you. For, lo, I raise up the Chaldeans, that bitter
and hasty nation, which shall march through the
breadth of the land, to possess the dwelling places
that are not theirs.* (Habakkuk 1:5–6)

The phrase "Behold you among the heathen" is an instruction for
Habakkuk to search among the non-Jewish nations of the world.
In doing so he would find God doing works that would cause a
person to "wonder marvelously." Such a search was in effect the
beginning of God's "reproving" Habakkuk.

3. Yet another problem with Habakkuk's prayer that commanded
God's correction was the fact he could not discern either that God
had heard or answered his prayer. This explains his words in 1:2:

*O LORD, how long shall I cry, and you will not
hear! even cry out unto you of violence, and you
will not save!* (Habakkuk 1:2)

Habakkuk's impeachment of God was the result of his prayer
being only the act of telling God what to do. Also, he had prese-
lected the time for God's answer to appear. By offering to God
these limited choices for answering prayer, he had placed God in
an untenable position. Since God could not remain sovereign and
respond positively to Habakkuk's prayer, Habakkuk was left with
no ability to discern if and when the answer had come. To say this
in another way: God could not be God and answer the prayer as
Habakkuk anticipated.

The conversation between God and Habakkuk recorded in chapter
1 left Habakkuk with the knowledge that impeaching God without

learning the truth about prayer had placed him in jeopardy of God's correction. Hebrews 12:5 shares this information with us:

And you have forgotten the exhortation which speaks unto you as unto children, "My son, despise not the chastening of the Lord, nor faint when you are rebuked of him: For whom the Lord loves he chastens, and scourges every son whom he receives. (Hebrews 12:5-6)

Habakkuk now knows that God is going teach him a lesson about how to pray. So Habakkuk moves to the tower to get himself above and away from the distractions that would hinder his learning and otherwise interfere with that which is happening between himself and God. Habakkuk is doing two things-*watching and waiting.*

He is no longer talking; instead he is listening.
He is no longer arguing; instead he is submitting.
He is no longer complaining; instead he is looking.
He is no longer impeaching God; instead he is waiting for God to "reprove" him.

But they that wait upon the LORD shall renew their strength; they shall mount up with wings as eagles; they shall run, and not be weary; and they shall walk, and not faint. (Isaiah 40:31)

It is good that a man should both hope and quietly wait for the salvation of the LORD. (Lamentations 3:26)

Both watching and waiting are essential to prayer. While we wait for God to answer, we watch for the answer. If we wait and do not watch, the answer may come and not be recognized. If we watch and do not wait, we will get frustrated with what we assume to be a non-answer, or maybe a delay, on God's part. Never become irritable while waiting. If you patiently wait and watch, you will find that you can wait much faster.

The "tower" location is a very significant matter. The towers were strategically located in the area where the action was most likely to occur. The books of 2 Chronicles and Nehemiah give much emphasis to the building and use of towers. There are several areas (towers) where a person can most likely see God at work. A partial list would include the individual person, the family, the church, the community, the country, and the world. The nature of the prayer (burden) request will help determine where the "tower" is located.

The following verses of chapter 2 give a prophecy of God's judgment upon Babylon and a description of the downfall of the nation. One needs to remember and follow the train of conversation between Habakkuk and God concerning Babylon.

Chapter 1:6–11 is God's statement of the negative characteristics of Babylon which make her a suitable instrument for God's use in bringing judgment upon Judah.

Chapter 1:14–17 records Habakkuk's derogatory statements about Babylon and their effect upon persons like himself.

Chapter 2:3–20 is God's prophetic word to Habakkuk about the downfall of Babylon. These verses also trace the pathway and activities by which Babylon became so rich and powerful. At least a century before Habakkuk's prayer and God's judgment upon Babylon, Isaiah had prophesied that such would happen to that nation. In Isaiah 13:19–22 we read:

> *And Babylon, the glory of kingdoms, the beauty of the Chaldees' excellency, shall be as when God overthrew Sodom and Gomorrah. It shall never be inhabited, neither shall it be dwelt in from generation to generation: neither shall the Arabian pitch tent there; neither shall the shepherds make their fold there. But wild beasts of the desert shall lie there; and their houses shall be full of doleful creatures; and owls shall dwell there, and satyrs shall dance there. And the wild beasts of the islands shall cry in their desolate houses, and dragons in their pleasant palaces: and her time is near to come, and her days shall not be prolonged.*

Isaiah's prophecy continues in chapter 47 with a more detailed description of the fate of the city and nation of Babylon.

Jeremiah joins Habakkuk and Isaiah in a prophecy of the fall of Babylon. In chapter 50 and 51, he gives a more specific account as to which will be the nation to bring about the collapse of Babylon. Jeremiah predicts the fall of Babylon into the hands of the Medes and the Persians. Daniel 5 gives record of the event of the fall of the nation in the days of Nebuchadnezzar and Belshazzar.

Some students of prophecy see in Revelation 17–18 the fulfillment of Isaiah's prophecy. These two chapters in Revelation also seem to have a lot in common with the prophecy of Habakkuk 2.

Also, Revelation 18 has much in common with the prophecies of Isaiah. But in Revelation 18 the emphasis is upon economics or world commerce, perhaps contemporary with the fall of Babylon of the last days.

However, it is the opinion of some students that Babylon of the Revelation is in fact the world (worldly) system of government and commerce that becomes fully grown in the last days. In support of this view is the thinking of many that the next great famine will not be one of food and want. It will rather be a famine of money with which to buy what a person needs to sustain life. The resources will be available-such as food, clothing, and shelter-but there will be no money available with which to purchase these items. It is thought that the worldly economy and its banking system will have failed and that there will be no such thing as money. This is indicated by the crying of the kings and merchants in Revelation 18:10–11.

> *Standing afar off for the fear of her torment, saying, Alas, alas, that great city Babylon, that mighty city! for in one hour is thy judgment come. [11] And the merchants of the earth shall weep and mourn over her; for no man buys their merchandise anymore.*

PRECEPT # 11
Lessons learned from God's rebuke call for a testimony.

But we return to Habakkuk 2 and continue our study of what he learned when he went to a watchtower to see God at work and was subsequently "reproved" by God. Habakkuk receives God's instructions about his choice to become a "watchman." God says these things to Habakkuk about the answer to his prayer that He has planned.

A. The answer will be clear: *And the LORD answered me, and said, Write the vision, and make it plain upon tables, that he may run that reads it* (v.2).

B. God wants this answer to be permanently recorded, because future generations are going to need it. God says, "Write it down. And write it plainly."

The revelation (literally *vision*) was to be recorded on tablets so God's word would be preserved and, even more importantly, publicized, so that a herald could read and understand clearly and fully the contents of the message. This phrase has been understood and interpreted in two ways. Some understand it to mean that the vision is to be recorded in such a way that it could be read and remembered by a person who is speedily passing by. The idea, as interpreted by this view, is that the recording is to be of such nature that a messenger "may read it on the run." This would probably require clear, large letters with much "white space." The messenger would be able to read the tablet on the run without the delay of having to stop to determine the details or verify the content.

The church of which I was pastor had joined with the other Baptist churches of the local association to plan and promote an evangelistic campaign. Plans had been made to use the local college football stadium as the venue for the crusade. The planning committee had asked me to serve as publicity director for the event. The editor of the local newspaper was asked to serve on the publicity committee with me. I met with him in his office for a preliminary planning time. As we talked about how much publicity our budget could purchase, he began to explain what was available. He explained about one-column ads, two-column ads, etc. He spoke of quarter-page ads, half-page ads, and full-page ads. Then we began to discuss the matter of copy for the ads. It was then that he made a statement that stopped me short. I had to ask him to explain what he meant. He spoke of "white space." His statement was: "People read the white space." He explained that if too much copy was put on a page, there would be too little "white space" for the page to be easily read. The "white space" allows for the page to be quickly and easily read. That is comparable to what God was saying to Habakkuk in 2:2: "Make it easy to read."

> *And the LORD answered me, and said, Write the vision, and make it plain upon tables, that he may run that readeth it.*

Another possible explanation of the verse is that the message would be recorded so clearly and detailed that the herald could read it and learn exactly what had happened. The idea, as interpreted by this view, is that the recording is to be of such a nature that a messenger could "run after reading" and be confident that he had the necessary facts and could correctly deliver the message to others. In the Bible, 2 Samuel 18 records an incident that may help us understand this idea.

> *Then said Ahimaaz the son of Zadok, Let me now run, and bear the king tidings, how that the LORD has avenged him of his enemies. And Joab said unto him, You shall not bear tidings this day, but you shall bear tidings another day: but this day*

you shall bear no tidings, because the king's son is dead. Then said Joab to Cushi, Go tell the king what you have seen. And Cushi bowed himself unto Joab and ran. Then said Ahimaaz the son of Zadok yet again to Joab, But, howsoever, let me, I pray you, also run after Cushi. And Joab said, Wherefore, will you run, my son, seeing that you have no tidings ready? But howsoever, said he, let me run. And he said unto him, Run. Then Ahimaaz ran by the way of the plain and overran Cushi. And David sat between the two gates: and the watchman went up to the roof over the gate unto the wall, and lifted up his eyes, and looked, and behold a man running alone. And the watchman cried and told the king. And the king said, If he be alone, there is tidings in his mouth. And he came apace and drew near. And the watchman saw another man running: and the watchman called unto the porter, and said, Behold, another man running alone. And the king said, He also bring tidings. And the watchman said, Me thinks the running of the foremost is like the running of Ahimaaz the son of Zadok. And the king said, He is a good man, and cometh with good tidings. And Ahimaaz called, and said unto the king, All is well. And he fell down to the earth upon his face before the king, and said, Blessed, be the LORD your God, which has delivered up the men that lifted up their hand against my lord the king. And the king said, Is the young man Absalom safe? And Ahimaaz answered, When Joab sent the king's servant, and me your servant, I saw a great tumult, but I knew not what it was. And the king

*said unto him, Turn aside, and stand here. And he
turned aside and stood still. And, behold, Cushi
came; and Cushi said, Tidings, my lord the king:
for the LORD has avenged you this day of all them
that rose up against you. And the king said unto
Cushi, Is the young man Absalom safe? And Cushi
answered, The enemies of my lord the king, and
all that rise against you to do you hurt, be as that
young man is. And the king was much moved, and
went up to the chamber over the gate, and wept:
and as he went, thus he said, O my son Absalom,
my son, my son Absalom! would God I had died
for you, O Absalom, my son, my son!*

The lesson to be seen in this story is that Ahimaaz had not actually
been an eyewitness to what happened to Absalom. Therefore, he
requested and was reluctantly given permission to run as a messenger to David without having a message of any sure substance.
He could share no details that would be helpful to the king. Cushi,
on the other hand, was an eyewitness to the Absalom event. He
possessed correct, complete, and verifiable information. He had
seen in detail what had happened in the battle. He was qualified
to run as a messenger.

The application is that Habakkuk is instructed to write what he
sees God doing and make it so clear that the messenger can read,
comprehend, and remember what had happened. The messenger
could then run with a verifiable message. The real lesson is: "Don't
impeach the integrity of God by accusing Him of being unrespon-
sive to prayer unless or until you have a firsthand, objective, and
unobstructed view of the scene of action and have discovered
exactly what God is or is not doing." Then, and only then, are

you qualified to serve as a messenger to share information about God's response to prayer.

The writer of several of the Psalms was quick to give testimony about God's answer to prayer. It will be noticed as one reads the following excerpts that the writers are very careful to state clearly and exactly the way God answered prayer. That is what Habakkuk is instructed to do when God rebukes him for making false charges complaining that God was neither hearing nor answering his prayer.

I cried unto the LORD with my voice, And he heard me out of his holy hill. Selah. (Psalm 3:4)

I sought the LORD, and he heard me,
And delivered me from all my fears.
They looked unto him, and were lightened:
And their faces were not ashamed. (Psalm 34:4-5)

I waited patiently for the LORD; And he inclined unto me, and heard my cry. He brought me up also out of an horrible pit, out of the miry clay, And set my feet upon a rock, and established my goings. And he hath put a new song in my mouth, even praise unto our God: Many shall see it, and fear, and shall trust in the LORD. (Psalm 40:1-3)

Each believer who offers a prayer to God should have a "watch-tower" from which to see God answer prayer. This will enable God's answers to be clearly seen and plainly recorded. The value of assurance harvested from answered prayer can provide the believer with immeasurable strength. It will also become a strong incentive to future and frequent times of prayer and fellowship with God. The believer can then follow God's instructions for recording a testimony of answered prayer: "Write the vision, and make it plain upon tables, that he may run that reads it."

God had the answer scheduled before Habakkuk prayed (v. 3):

> *For the vision is yet for an appointed time, but at the end it shall speak, and not lie: though it tarry, wait for it; because it will surely come, it will not tarry.*

PRECEPT # 12
Delaying the answer is not denying the answer.

Remember the vision was the burden and the burden was God's coming judgment upon Judah. God's plans for the judgment of Judah would be understood at the appointed time, and the plan would be activated at the appointed time.

The word for "appointed time" (*mo'ed*–לְמוֹעֵד) is used for both an appointed time and an appointed place. Both time and place, however, have in mind a meeting between two or more persons. I write this on Good Friday 2019, and my thought is of the experience of the disciples who walked and talked with Jesus on the road to Emmaus after his resurrection. Their evaluation of that time of fellowship is recorded in Luke 24:32: "And they said one to another, Did not our heart burn within us, while he talked with us by the way, and while he opened to us the scriptures?"

The meaning of "at the end" (*qets*–קֵץ) seems to refer to a "designated goal"-not simply the extremity but a conclusion toward which something proceeds.

The "appointed time" could refer to the conclusion as far as time is concerned. While "at the end" may refer to the outcome or the effect of the vision. The idea is that after the timely conclusion of the things contained in the vision, there will be a message-a lesson learned-from the events contained in the vision.

Though it tarry... it will not tarry

This seems to be a self-contradicting statement. It could be considered an oxymoron. It literally reads: "though it delay it will not delay," and it simply means this: Though the timing is not ours and there seems to be a delay-a tardiness-in the fulfillment of the vision, it is not a delay in God's timing. What seems like a delay to us is not a delay with God. He is in control. These are not, nor will there ever be, random circumstances in God's schedule. God is always on time. The classic illustration of this truth is found in Galatians 4:4-5:

> *But when the fullness of the time was come, God sent forth his Son, made of a woman, made under the law, to redeem them that were under the law, that we might receive the adoption of sons.*

The phrase to note is "the fullness of time." God always acts at the right time -the "appointed time."

God's sovereignty over time is easily seen in the gospel of John. In that New Testament book, there is a record of seven times when Jesus is seen to have complete control of time as the gospel ddescribes his journey toward the cross and death and resurrection. I will not at this time and place give details of this truth about John's gospel. The reader can read that gospel and discover this information. The "appointed time" for Jesus is revealed to us in John 12:23-33. Nothing *just happens* with God. All things are planned. Read Ecclesiastes 3 and learn that "To everything there is a season, and a time to every purpose under the heaven." Every prayer offered to God has a preplanned answer and a preplanned time for that answer to happen.

> *And it shall come to pass, that before they call, I will answer; and while they are yet speaking, I will hear.* (Isaiah 65:24)

Karen Peck and the southern gospel music group New River sing a song titled "Four Days Late and Still on Time." The song is based on the story recorded in John 11 about the death and resurrection of Lazarus. Jesus waited four days after he had heard of the illness of Lazarus before going to Bethany. The sisters, Mary and Martha, said to Jesus upon his "late" arrival: "If you had been here our brother had not died." But Jesus simply said: "Your brother shall live again." The point being that although Jesus, according to the sisters, came four days late, he was still on time.

Again, this axiom is repeated: There are no random circumstances. God is sovereign and is always on time. And that which God plans always happens on time–"the appointed time." "Though it tarry... it will not tarry." God's answer to prayer is never late, never delayed beyond His appointed time. It is always on time. To Habakkuk it seemed that God was neither listening nor answering his prayer. From his vantage point on the tower, he learned that God always answers and always answers on time. And that is the heart of the message in the book of Habakkuk!

Several biblical illustrations can be cited to show a pattern in God's schedule of events. They always show God to be on time, every time. One illustration is that of the experience of Nehemiah. The events described in Nehemiah take place after the seventy years of Judah being in captivity in Babylon. Babylon has been judged and the Persians are now the dominant world power. Nehemiah 1:1 gives details of how he heard from one of his brothers of the deplorable conditions being endured by the few inhabitants residing in Jerusalem. The news came to him in the Jewish month Chisleu while he was still in captivity and serving as "cupbearer" to King Artaxerxes. The news immediately became a burden to him and he began praying. Nehemiah 1:4 informs us that he immediately "sat down and wept, and mourned certain days, and fasted, and prayed before the God of heaven." He prayed and fasted in this manner for a period of three months or more. Chapter 2:1 tells us that it was not until the month Nisan that the king observed a change in him. It was then that he spoke to the king about Jerusalem. God had already inspired Jeremiah to prophesy about the seventy years of captivity. In fact, we can be quite certain that Jeremiah was deported to Babylon. Habakkuk's experience of burdened prayer and his complaint about God's refusal, or at least his delay, in answering, must be dated prior to the actual fall of Jerusalem and the deportation of the Jews to Babylon. Therefore, Nehemiah's prayer and what seems to be an apparent delay on God's part to answer must be dated after the seventy years had run their course. Nehemiah in many ways shared an experience similar to Habakkuk. God may have also said to him:

For the vision is yet for an appointed time, but at the end it shall speak, and not lie: though it tarry, wait for it; because it will surely come, it will not tarry."

Daniel's experience is yet another classic illustration of this truth. Daniel tells us that in the first year of the reign of Darius he learned that God's plan was for the duration of the captivity to be a period of seventy years. He had, while himself in captivity, obtained-how we are not told-a copy of Jeremiah's prophecy. After careful study he discovered the time frame for the captivity (Daniel 9:2). Upon making this discovery, he writes: "I set my face unto the LORD my God, to seek by prayer and supplication, with fasting, and sackcloth, and ashes; And I prayed unto the LORD my God, and made my confession." After such praying, Gabriel came to him and verified what he had discovered from his study of Jeremiah (Daniel 9:21ff).

Again, in the third year of the reign of Cyrus, king of Persia, it was revealed to Daniel that what he had discovered was true, but the appointed time was long. Daniel understood what the vision meant (Daniel 10:1). He became mournful and started fasting–a fast and prayer time that continued for "three full weeks." It was then that he saw "Michael, one of the chief princes." Daniel was so overcome by the appearance of Michael that, being alone, he lost his strength and fell into a deep sleep. A hand touched Daniel and raised him up. Michael then indicated that he had been dispatched twenty-one days earlier to communicate God's answer to Daniel's prayer. But now he communicates that answer to Daniel.

For the vision is yet for an appointed time, but at the end it shall speak, and not lie: though it tarry, wait for it; because it will surely come, it will not tarry.

God is always on time! Every time!

God's answer is definite.

> *For the vision is yet for an appointed time, but at*
> *the end it shall speak, and not lie: though it tarry,*
> *wait for it; because it will surely come, it will not*
> *tarry. (v. 3).*

The root of the word meaning "shall speak" (*puwach* -וְיָפֵחַ) means "to breathe or to exhale." A messenger is pictured who has seen and read (see v.2) that which he knows to be an extremely important message. He has it, so to speak, "bottled up" inside himself. There is a schedule, an appointed time, for each event described in the message to take place. The message is so important that at the appointed time the messenger "speaks" or "exhales" its truth.

God said that he would speak "and not lie" (*kazab* -יְכַזֵּב) This word carries the meaning of "to lie, tell a lie, be a liar." The prophet Habakkuk and all who read his book are being told that God can be trusted to do exactly what He promised. Every prophetic event contained in the vision will come to pass in God's own time.

God said in Psalm 89:34-35:

> *My covenant will I not break, nor alter the thing*
> *that is gone out of my lips. Once have I sworn by*
> *my holiness that I will not lie unto David.*

In these verses we discover three things that God says:

1. I will do what I said I would do: *My covenant will I not break.*

2. I will not change my commitment: *Nor alter the thing that is gone out of my lips.*

3. I will not lie about it: *I have sworn by my holiness that I will not lie to David.*

Additional reinforcement is given to the concept of God's veracity in Hebrews 6:13- 20:

> *For when God made promise to Abraham, because he could swear by no greater, he swore by himself, Saying, Surely, blessing I will bless thee, and multiplying I will multiply thee. And so, after he had patiently endured, he obtained the promise. For men verily swear by the greater: and an oath for confirmation is to them an end of all strife. Wherein God, willing more abundantly to shew unto the heirs of promise the immutability of his counsel, confirmed it by an oath: That by two immutable things, in which it was impossible for God to lie, we might have a strong consolation, who have fled for refuge to lay hold upon the hope set before us: Which hope we have as an anchor of the soul, both sure and steadfast, and which enters into that within the veil; Whither the forerunner is for us entered, even Jesus, made an high priest for ever after the order of Melchisedec.*

The Hebrew passage is telling us that God has put Himself under "oath," that He will not lie when His covenant is involved. He has sworn by two immutable witnesses that He is speaking the truth, making it impossible for Him to lie.

To question God's answer is to question God's character. God's answer is to be accepted by faith.

Behold, his soul which is lifted up is not upright in him: but the just shall live by his faith" (v.4).

The conversation at this point returns to speaking of Babylon. In 1:6 God had revealed to Habakkuk that Babylon was to be his instrument to bring judgment to Judah. God then speaks of the characteristics of Babylon that make that nation suitable to use for this purpose. Habakkuk responds to God by describing Babylon from the standpoint of how that nation has characteristics that have a very negative and destructive effect upon him. Nevertheless, Habakkuk has taken a position of advantage that will allow him to see clearly what God is doing. God instructs him to maintain a record of what he discovers and to write clearly so that the record can be read; then the readers can go on their journey with a full understanding of God's actions and will be equipped to share the message.

Now, in 2:4ff God reveals to Habakkuk what will happen to Babylon after that nation has served as His instrument of judgment. This is the third section of prophecy in the book of Habakkuk, the others being 1:5-11 and 1:14-17.[3]

Habakkuk 2.5 injects this into the conversation:

Yes also, because he transgresses by wine, he is a proud man, neither keeps at home, who enlarges his desire as hell, and is as death, and cannot be satisfied, but gathers unto him all nations, and heaps unto him all people.

---

[3] Additional study of Habakkuk 2:4 and other classic statements made by Habakkuk will be included in a later part of this book.

The first part of this verse gives a general description of a nation using wine in excess. Wine generates a false sense of well-being and fosters pride. It produces negligence in responsibility to the home. It is also presented as the root cause of "transgression," which must have some implication as to a general disregard for law and order. Babylon is seen in other Scripture references as abusing the use of wine. In Daniel 5 Babylon was conquered while Belshazzar, and perhaps other government officials, was having a riotous feast with an abundance of wine being consumed.

Wine is seen in this verse as either the cause of, or the result of, abnormal pride on the part of Babylon. In 1:7; 1:10; and 2:4, 5, there are several references to the pride of Babylon. Here that pride seems to be the source of greed. The nation is said to be "as greedy as the grave." Death and the grave are never satisfied. Proverbs 27:20 tells us that:

> *Hell and destruction are never full; so the eyes of man are never satisfied.*

Babylon, according to 1:17, sought to take "captive all the peoples." She opened wide her insatiable mouth to devour all peoples. But this evil nation would not continue unpunished. God's judgment would bring her to fall!

Chapter 2:5 also contains a significant statement that is a very clear description of the Babylonian culture, especially of its leaders. That statement -"he is a proud man"—could either refer to the male population of Babylon or it could be a more specific reference to Nebuchadnezzar himself. It may have reference to both. Nebuchadnezzar had assumed the throne of Babylon in 605. He initiated a series of attacks on Judah and Jerusalem, and in

597 he overthrew Jerusalem. The ruler of Judah, Jehoiachin, and many citizens of Judah were exiled to Babylon. Nebuchadnezzar destroyed the temple of the Jews in 586 and deported others to Babylon. There possibly were other deportations in 582 or 581.

Daniel 1- 4 is a biographical record of some of the actions of Nebuchadnezzar. The focus is upon his dreams and visions, which were interpreted by Daniel. In Daniel 4:28 -37 there is a story recorded that gives in bold detail the pride that filled his heart. Verse 30 says:

> *The king spoke, and said: "Is not this great Babylon, that I have built for the house of the kingdom by the might of my power, and for the honor of my majesty.*

His pride clearly shows through the words of his mouth recorded here. Perhaps every reader of this book will have heard the sage advice, "Do not interrupt another's conversation." In Daniel 4:31 the action of interrupting another person's conversation is most clearly demonstrated. Read Daniel's description of the event:

> *While the word was in the king's mouth, there fell a voice from heaven, saying, O king Nebuchadnezzar, to you it is spoken; The kingdom is departed from you. And they shall drive you from men, and your dwelling shall be with the beasts of the field: they shall make you to eat grass as oxen, and seven times shall pass over you, until you know that the Most High rules in the kingdom of men, and gives it to whomsoever he will.* (Daniel 4:31)

Apparently the "seven times" mentioned here is to be understood as meaning seven years. Daniel 4 goes on to describe how these words were fulfilled. At the end Nebuchadnezzar said: "Now I Nebuchadnezzar praise and extol and honor the King of heaven, all whose works are truth, and his ways judgment: and those who walk in pride he is able to abase."

This story of Nebuchadnezzar demonstrates the truth of Proverbs 16:18: "Pride goes before destruction, and a haughty spirit before a fall." They may also be recorded as a reminder to each succeeding generation that pride is a very destructive attitude and is one of which God disapproves. Proverbs 6:16-19 speaks to this truth:

> *These six things does the LORD hate: yes, seven are an abomination unto him: A proud look, a lying tongue, and hands that shed innocent blood, An heart that devises wicked imaginations, feet that be swift in running to mischief. A false witness that speaks lies, and he who sows discord among brethren.*

As a matter of record, it can be said that the insatiable appetite of Babylon for world conquest and power was fueled by pride. Again Proverbs 13:10 states that:

> *Only by pride comes contention: but with the well advised is wisdom.*

God used the pride of Babylon to make that nation his instrument of judgment upon Judah for their sins, and he then judged that same sin that was so very prevalent in Babylon.

Chapter Eight

A Mocking Poem!

Habakkuk 2:5-20

Yes also, because he transgresses by wine, he is a proud man, neither keeps at home, who enlarges his desire as hell, and is as death, and cannot be satisfied, but gathers unto him all nations, and heaps unto him all people: Shall not all these take up a parable against him, and a taunting proverb against him, and say, Woe to him that increases that which is not his! how long? and to him that lades himself with thick clay! Shall they not rise up suddenly that shall bite you, and awake that shall vex you, and you shalt be for booties unto them? Because you have spoiled many nations, all the remnant of the people shall spoil you; because of men's blood, and for the violence of the land, of the city, and of all that dwell therein. Woe to him that covets an evil covetousness to his house, that he may set his nest on high, that he may be delivered from the power of evil! You have consulted shame to your house by cutting off many people and have sinned against your soul. For the stone shall cry out of the wall, and the beam out of the timber shall answer it. Woe to him that builds a town with blood and establishes a city by iniquity! Behold, is it not of the LORD of hosts that the people shall labor in the very fire, and the people shall weary themselves for very vanity? For the earth shall be filled with the knowledge of the glory of the LORD, as the waters cover the sea.

Woe unto him that gives his neighbor drink, that puts your bottle to him, and makes him drunken also, that you may look on their nakedness! You are filled with shame for glory: drink you also, and let your foreskin be uncovered: the cup of the LORD'S right hand shall be turned unto you and shameful spewing shall be on thy glory. For the violence of Lebanon shall cover you, and the spoil of beasts, which made them afraid, because of men's blood, and for the violence of the land, of the city, and of all that dwell therein. What profits the graven image that the maker thereof has graven it; the molten image, and a teacher of lies, that the maker of his work trusts therein, to make dumb idols? Woe unto him that saith to the wood, Awake; to the dumb stone, Arise, it shall teach! Behold, it is laid over with gold and silver, and there is no breath at all in the midst of it. But the LORD is in his holy temple: let all the earth keep silence before him.

Beginning with Habakkuk 2:6 there is recorded "a parable" or "a taunting proverb" against Babylon. This can be seen as one song with five verses (6-8, 9-11, 12-14, 15-18, and 19-20) or it can be viewed as five songs, each being sung by a different entity or different sections of a choir. Either view presents each verse (song) as dealing with an issue that contributes to the downfall of Babylon. Each verse (song) begins with the word *Woe* (הוֹי–*howy*) an expression of distress pronounced in the face of impending disaster or in view of coming judgment (compare Isaiah 3:11, 5:11, and 10:5) or because of certain sins. The word is used frequently by the prophets.

The first verse (song) is found in 2:6-8 and has to do with greediness.

> *Shall not all these take up a parable against him,*
> *and a taunting proverb against him, and say, Woe*
> *to him that increases that which is not his! how*
> *long? and to him that loads himself with thick clay!*
> *Shall they not rise up suddenly that shall bite you,*
> *and awake that shall vex you, and you shall be for*
> *booties unto them? Because you have spoiled many*
> *nations, all the remnant of the people shall spoil*
> *you; because of men's blood, and for the violence*
> *of the land, of the city, and of all that dwell therein.*

Babylon had swiftly and harshly conquered many nations and in doing so had just as swiftly and mercilessly accumulated significant wealth. An example of this is the fact that when Babylon conquered Jerusalem, Nebuchadnezzar transported all the gold vessels and instruments of the temple to Babylon. This in itself amounted to significant wealth. The story is recounted in 2 Chronicles 36.

The prophecy of this section is that just as swiftly as Babylon made herself rich by the conquest of other nations, the nations would suddenly awake and arise and spoil Babylon. Babylon would become "booties" (spoil or plunder) for those nations. The well-worn cliché "What goes around comes around" would be Babylon's experience.

The next verse (song) is in 2:9-1 and has covetousness for its theme.

> *Woe to him that covets an evil covetousness to his house, that he may set his nest on high, that he may be delivered from the power of evil! You have consulted shame to your house by cutting off many people and have sinned against your soul. For the stone shall cry out of the wall, and the beam out of the timber shall answer it.*

Babylon is characterized in these verses as being covetous beyond the usual level. Hers was an "evil covetousness." It was the thinking of Babylon that by acquiring wealth she would "set his nest on high" and become inaccessible to any enemy. The *evil covetousness* was desired in order to be *delivered from the power of evil*. The word for *evil* is (רַע -ra) and is thought by some students of the Bible to be derived from the Hebrew word that means "to break, smash, crush." If this is the correct derivation, it would imply that *ra* connotes sin in the sense of destructive hurtfulness. Such would lead us to understand that Babylon intended to harm and bring hurt and suffering upon the captured nations.

If this was indeed the intent of Babylon, v.10 reveals that Babylon had "consulted shame to your house by cutting off many people." The word *consulted* means "to counsel." Babylon had adopted the shameful philosophy of *cutting off* (the word comes from a root that means "to annihilate") *many people*. This practice caused Habakkuk to say that Babylon *hast sinned against thy soul*. This statement may mean that she had put herself in jeopardy.

The prophecy of this section is that the course of action chosen by Babylon would return to haunt the nation and ultimately result in its downfall.

The third verse (song) is contained in 2:12-14, and *iniquity* is the word used to describe the sins of Babylon.

> *Woe to him that builds a town with blood and establishes a city by iniquity! Behold, is it not of the LORD of hosts that the people shall labor in the very fire, and the people shall weary themselves for very vanity? For the earth shall be filled with the knowledge of the glory of the LORD, as the waters cover the sea.*

In 2:11which may be intended as a transition from the preceding verse (song):

> *For the stone shall cry out of the wall, and the beam out of the timber shall answer it.*

This metaphor may be used to introduce the matter of building a town and establishing a city. If so, verses 12-14 contain the "cries" of "wall" and "timbers."

Verse 12 States, "Woe to him that builds with blood" (דם *-dam*) an act by which a human life is taken, or blood is shed). The word can also mean "blood that is shed by violence." The iniquity being referenced is nothing short of murder. Babylon's cities and infrastructure were built by slave labor with little or no regard for the number of slaves who died in the process. Resulting from the construction projects were murder, bloodshed, oppression, and tyranny. Babylon proved to be a very cruel taskmaster, indeed.

Verse 13 declares that the course of action outlined in 2:12 is not in keeping with the character and laws of God, who is the Lord of Hosts. Several translations see this verse describing the work of the slaves as being "fuel for the fire." It would be of short duration and was an exercise in futility. Instead of having a nation filled with the production of slave labor, Babylon (and all others) would discover a world "filled with the knowledge of the glory of the LORD, as the waters cover the sea."

This statement found in v. 14 will be discussed later because of the significance of its content. Herein is found the prophetic element of these verses in Habakkuk. When Babylon is judged, the knowledge of it will be worldwide. Everyone will know about it. So extensive and abundant will be that knowledge that it will cover the earth like the water of the sea.

The fourth verse (song) is found in 2:15-17 and has *immorality* for its theme.

> *Woe unto him that gives his neighbor drink, that puts his bottle to him, and makes him drunken also, that you may look on their nakedness! You are filled with shame for glory: you drink also, and let your uncircumcision be uncovered: the cup of the LORD'S right hand shall be turned unto you, and shameful spewing shall be on your glory. For the violence of Lebanon shall cover you, and the spoil of beasts, which made them afraid, because*

of men's blood, and for the violence of the land, of
the city, and of all that dwell therein.

The various immoral actions described here have their birth in the abuse of wine. Habakkuk 2:5 has made reference to Babylon's propensity for wine and drunkenness.

In v. 15 one person is seen to cause another to drink too much wine and become drunk, and they expose themselves in lewd ways. In doing so the fact that they are uncircumcised is revealed. This certainly refers to the physical act of circumcision but could easily speak of their spiritual condition as well. In this later sense, it would reveal their lack of a covenant relationship with God. The conduct described in 2:15 calls to mind a later word written by the Apostle Paul in Philippians 3:18-19:

> *For many walk, of whom I have told you often, and*
> *now tell you even weeping, that they are the ene-*
> *mies of the cross of Christ: Whose end is destruc-*
> *tion, whose God is their belly, and whose glory is*
> *in their shame, who mind earthly things.*

The last line of 2:16 speaks of "shameful spewing" (קִיקָלוֹן–*qiy-qalown*) using an emphatic form in Hebrew (used only here in the OT) that signifies extreme contempt. The once-glorious Babylon was pictured as a disgraceful, contemptible drunk.

The fifth and final verse (song) of Habakkuk 2 is in 2:18-20 and has *idolatry* for its subject.

> *What profits the graven image that the maker*
> *thereof has graven it; the molten image, and a*

teacher of lies that the maker of his work trusts therein, to make dumb idols? Woe unto him that says to the wood, Awake; to the dumb stone, Arise, it shall teach! Behold, it is laid over with gold and silver, and there is no breath at all in the midst of it. But the LORD is in his holy temple: let all the earth keep silence before him.

Verse 2:18 asks a very appropriate question when the subject is *idolatry*: "What is the value of an idol?" The verse seems to refer to an object cast of metal while the next verse refers to an object carved of wood. Whether cast or carved, neither the process nor the material of which the idol is made changes the answer to Habakkuk's question. His answer is that the idol is an object that is a "teacher of lies," for people were deceived and deluded by it, thinking it could help them.

Verse 2:19 shows the absurdity of a person saying to a piece of wood, "Come to life!" or to a lifeless bit of stone, "Wake up!" when there is absolutely no breath in the object.

Verse 2:20 contrasts the LORD with the idols described in 2:18-19. In verse 20 God said to Habakkuk: "But the LORD is in his holy temple: let all the earth keep silence before him." Habakkuk had introduced the character of God in 1:12-13. He will issue a follow-up to this verse with another statement about the magnitude and majesty of the LORD in 3:3-6. The point being made is that instead of shouting "Arise! Awake!" to a dumb idol, the whole earth must stand in silent awe and worship God. The Hebrew word rendered "be silent" (hāsâh -סה) means "hush" and speaks of the silence of awe and reverence. For Habakkuk, the message of 2:20 is clear:

"Stop complaining! Stop doubting! God is not indifferent to sin. He is not insensitive to suffering. Neither is he paralyzed by the horror of the magnitude of sin in Babylon and Judah. And the Lord is not inactive in the presence of such godless conduct. In His perfect time God will act in accordance with his character and divine purpose. Habakkuk, along with the rest of the world, is instructed to stand in a silent, hushed expectancy of God's intervention."

Chapter Nine

The Lord Is In His Holy Temple

Habakkuk 2:4, 14, 20

Behold, his soul which is lifted up is not upright in him: but the just shall live by his faith. (2:4)

For the earth shall be filled with the knowledge of the glory of the LORD, as the waters cover the sea. (2:14)

But the LORD is in his holy temple: let all the earth keep silence before him. (2:20)

H istory records that after the death of Nebuchadnezzar, the Babylonian empire rapidly declined. In a series of violent internal coups, several members of the dynasty succeeded each other. Nabonidus eventually imposed some stability, though several states broke away. The Belshazzar about whom we read in Daniel 5 was the son of Nabonidus. Nebuchadnezzar is said in Daniel 5:2 to be the father of Belshazzar. This appears to be true only in the sense that he was his "ancestor" or "predecessor," which is a use of the word elsewhere.

Daniel's account makes it clear that the Persian army was outside the walls of the city as Belshazzar brought up the golden goblets that had been taken from the temple in Jerusalem for use in his drunken orgy of self-indulgence. Belshazzar obviously felt that the city was impervious to assault. Daniel 4-5 causes one to realize that Belshazzar's purpose in using these specific vessels was to repudiate what his "father," Nebuchadnezzar, had learned about the living God. Perhaps Belshazzar thought that Babylon's fortunes had declined because of the relative neglect of the pagan deities. Nebuchadnezzar had learned to revere the God of Israel; Belshazzar was happy to spit in his eye. So they drank from the goblets and "praised the gods of gold and silver, of bronze, iron, wood and stone" (Daniel 5:4). Daniel sees the connection between the two emperors, and this forms part of his stinging rebuke. Belshazzar knew what "the Most High God" had done to Nebuchadnezzar, and how Nebuchadnezzar had come to his senses and acknowledged "that the Most High God is sovereign over the kingdoms of men and sets over them anyone he wishes"-and yet he set himself up "against the Lord of heaven" and refused to "honor the God who holds in his hand your life and all your ways" (Daniel 5:18-24). Somehow Belshazzar thought he could ignore or defy the God who had humbled his "father," Nebuchadnezzar, who was a far greater ruler than he could ever be.

So, what have we learned? Have we absorbed the lessons of history? That God will not, finally, be mocked or defied? That we are utterly dependent creatures, and if we fail to acknowledge this simple truth our sins are compounded? That God can humble and convert the most unlikely, like Nebuchadnezzar, and destroy those who defy him, like Belshazzar?

Although Habakkuk lived at least seventy years before the fall of Babylon and had the conversation with God that has become the

Bible book known as the "Prophecy of Habakkuk," he learned that God is always at work in the world around him. He learned that:

1. *"the just shall live by his faith."* (2:4)

2. *"the earth shall be filled with the knowledge of the glory of the LORD, as the waters cover the sea."* (2:14)

3. *"the LORD is in his holy temple: let all the earth keep silence before him."* (2:20)

The closing verse of this "song of woe" recorded by Habakkuk serves as a link to the "song of praise" that follows in Habakkuk 3. We will study that chapter later. But first we study Habakkuk 2:4, 14, and 20.

The pride of Babylon is indicated in 2:4. It seems that the pride is both the cause and a side effect of the success Babylon had experienced in conquering other nations. But that pride is described as producing a lack of righteousness in the soul of that nation. Babylon was apparently living by pride. This fact gives rise to Habakkuk's classic and often quoted phrase of 2:4: "The just shall live by his faith."

That statement made by Habakkuk is quoted three times in the New Testament. Habakkuk makes the statement in reference to those whose "soul... is lifted up is not upright in him." As previously mentioned, Habakkuk is speaking about Babylon and the pride-filled life adopted by that nation in the aftermath of world conquest. The general characteristic of citizens of Babylon is that they have a soul that is not "upright" in them. They have chosen not to follow God's guidelines while thinking they can live independently of God and succeed in life. Habakkuk is giving a prophetic statement about what is in the future for Babylon after the nation has been used as God's instrument of judgment against Judah. Contrasted with the prideful lifestyle of Babylon is the lifestyle ordained and approved by God—a lifestyle of faith.

Habakkuk 2:4 is quoted by the writer of Romans 1:17 in the context of a discussion of the revelation of God's righteousness: "For therein is the righteousness of God revealed from faith to faith: as it is written, the just shall live by faith." The essence of what Romans 1:17ff says is that God's righteousness is revealed to those who believe. Those who will not believe evolve into a lifestyle that is totally ungodly. Those who are "just" or (in the context of the passage) "righteous" choose to live by faith; that is to say, they become righteous by faith.

Habakkuk's statement is also quoted in Galatians 3:11. In that verse it is used in a discussion of how a person becomes right with God. Does a person become righteous by means of works or by faith? Abraham is cited as an example of how righteousness comes by and through faith.

> *Even as Abraham believed God, and it was accounted to him for righteousness. Know you therefore that they which are of faith, the same are the children of Abraham. And the scripture, foreseeing that God would justify the heathen through faith, preached before the gospel unto Abraham, saying, In you shall all nations be blessed. So then they which are of faith are blessed with faithful Abraham. For as many as are of the works of the law are under the curse: for it is written, 'Cursed is every one that continues not in all things which are written in the book of the law to do them. But*

that no man is justified by the law in the sight of God, it is evident: for, the just shall live by faith.

The conclusion reached by the writer of Galatians is that "no man is justified by the law in the sight of God, it is evident: for, the just shall live by faith." The word *law* is used as a synonym for *works*. The Habakkuk statement is used as proof that a person is saved by faith only.

Hebrews 10:38 is the third time the statement of Habakkuk is quoted in the New Testament. The other two New Testament quotations of Habakkuk are in the context of discussing how a person becomes right with God. The context here in Hebrews is very different. The writer here is not writing in reference to initial justification from sin. The subject is how to maintain a lifestyle that pleases God and does not "settle for less" than the best God has planned and promises to those who live by *faith*. In this passage the readers are urged to apply the principle of faith as they seek to grow spiritually. The readers are told that by putting their *faith in action* they can have a lifestyle pleasing to God in times of afflictions such as those described in Hebrews 10:32–34. Chapter 11 of Hebrews contains a list of persons who lived by faith. They fleshed out the principle of Habakkuk's declaration, "The just shall live by faith." And like those persons cited in chapter 11, the readers of Hebrews can live with assurance of the truth of God's promises. Faith gives life and vigor to them. They can trust God and live by faith and await His time, and as their faith maintains their spiritual life now, it shall be crowned with eternal life hereafter.

The Hebrews 10:38 quotation of Habakkuk is more in agreement with the originally intended application of Habakkuk's statement. Every principle and philosophy by which Babylon was living was contrary to God's word and will. But the *"just shall live by his faith."* It is understood that the faith being referenced here is faith in God. Such faith includes the existence of God, who God is, God's character, God's expressed guidelines for human conduct, etc.

Hebrews 11:1 expands our understanding of this principle where we are informed that: "Now faith is the substance of things hoped for, the evidence of things not seen." The word *substance* (ὑπόστασις) speaks about a foundation. This verse emphasizes the truth that faith in God is the foundational principle by which human life is to be governed and lived.

* * * * * * * * * *

Habakkuk chapters 1 and 2 record God answering prayer by using Babylon to judge Judah. The truth Habakkuk gleaned from Babylon's having been God's instrument in judgment and the ultimate downfall of Babylon is that the whole world will be filled with the *"knowledge of the glory of the LORD."*

> *For the earth shall be filled with the knowledge of the glory of the LORD, as the waters cover the sea.* (2:14)

Filled (מָלֵא–*male*) to fill, fulfill, overflow." Basically *male* means "to be full" in the sense of having something done to one. In 2 Kings 4:6, the word implies "to fill up": "And it came to pass, when the vessels were full, that she said..." The verb is sometimes used figuratively, as in Genesis 6:13 when God noted that "the earth is filled with violence." When used as a transitive verb, it means "the act or state of filling something." In Genesis 1:22

(the first occurrence of the word), God told the sea creatures to "Be fruitful, and multiply and fill the waters in the seas." *Male* can also mean "to fill up" in an exhaustive sense: "And the glory of the Lord filled the tabernacle" (Exodus 40:34).

Knowledge (דָּעָה–*yada*) Essentially the word means: (1) "to know by observing and reflecting (thinking)" and (2) "to know by experience." The first sense appears in Genesis 8:11, where Noah "knew" the waters had abated as a result of seeing the freshly picked olive leaf in the dove's mouth; he "knew" it after observing and thinking about what he had seen. He did not actually see or experience the abatement himself. In contrast to this knowing through reflection is the knowing that comes through experience with the senses, by investigation and proving, by reflection and consideration.

When y*ada* is used in an intensive or causative stem, it expresses a particular concept of revelation. God did not make Himself known by His name Jehovah to Abraham, Isaac, and Jacob. He did reveal that name to them and show that He was the God of the covenant. Nevertheless, the covenant was not fulfilled (they did not possess the Promised Land) until the time of Moses. The statement in Exodus 6:3 implies that now God was going to make Himself known "by His name." He was going to lead them to possess the land. God makes Himself known through revelatory acts, such as bringing judgment on the wicked (Psalm 9:16) and deliverance to His people (Isaiah 66:14). He also reveals Himself through the spoken word—for example, by the commands given through Moses (Ezekiel 20:11) and by promises such as those given to David (2 Samuel 7:21).

Glory (כָּבוֹד–*kabowd*) "honor; glory; great quantity; multitude; wealth; reputation [majesty]; splendor." *Kabod* can refer to the great physical weight or "quantity" of a thing. Sometimes the word refers to both "wealth" and a significant or positive "reputation."

The world, especially the nation of Judah, had grown weary of the proud boasting of Babylon. Now God has revealed to Habakkuk his plans for that nation and others like it that seek to acquire power and wealth while dishonoring the one true God. God's everlasting glory will fill the entire earth! The earth being filled with God's glory is spoken of in Isaiah 6:3:

> *And one cried unto another, and said, Holy, holy, holy, is the LORD of hosts: the whole earth is full of his glory.*

This verse also compares favorably with the declaration in Isaiah 11:9:

> *They shall not hurt nor destroy in all my holy mountain: for the earth shall be full of the knowledge of the LORD, as the waters cover the sea.*

Isaiah stated in 11:1-9 that the earth would be full of the knowledge of *the Lord*. Habakkuk stated that the earth would be filled with the knowledge of *the glory of the LORD*. Isaiah dealt with the essence of God. Habakkuk speaks of the revelation and knowledge of God's glory. Isaiah presented the fact, Habakkuk the knowledge of the fact. God will overthrow and judge all ungodly powers. The knowledge of the Lord's glory and majesty will be made evident and acknowledged throughout the earth.

* * * * * * * * * *

The second outgrowth of God's management of the world (*qodesh heykal*–בְּהֵיכַל קָדְשׁוֹ) is that people are left with no grounds for complaint or indictment of God (2:20).

> *But the LORD is in his holy temple: let all the earth keep silence before him.*

Holy (קֹדֶשׁ–*qodesh*) – "holiness; holy thing(s); sanctuary

Temple (הֵיכָל–*heykal*) -This word means "a palace." It sometimes is translated as "temple." When *hekal* means "temple," it will be indicated by two things: (1) the addition of "of the Lord" in some form of statement and (2) the use of the word *qodesh* (holy). Both of these markers are found here.

Silence (הָסָה–*hacah*)–This word is usually translated "be silent," "keep silent," "hold your peace," or "hold your tongue." God is telling Habakkuk that when he is finished with the work of judgment upon Babylon, it will be recognized that God is "in his holy temple"—a position of authority and supremacy—and the world will have no rebuttal of what He has accomplished. All peoples will be left speechless and will stand in awe in the knowledge of God's glory. In Habakkuk 1:5 God tells the prophet that the work he is doing throughout the world will cause him to *regard and wonder marvelously*. The prophet will be moved to a holy silence by the awesome works of God.

This triad of triumphant verses gives the believer so much incentive and inspiration for celebration. Deliverance by faith (2:4); living an abundant life by faith (2:4); living in the atmosphere of, and knowledge that, God is being glorified (2:14); sharing with

other believers in times of fellowship and worship of God in genuine praise and worship (2:20).

Habakkuk began chapter 1 complaining about God's ineptitude
and failure. He ended chapter 2 celebrating God's eternal faith-
fulness and greatness. The lessons he learned surpass evaluation.
They led him to write the song of *praise and prayer* recorded for
us in chapter 3.

Chapter Ten

A Prayer of Habakkuk

Habakkuk 3:1-19

A prayer of Habakkuk the prophet upon Shigionoth.

O LORD, I have heard your speech, and was afraid: O LORD, revive your work in the midst of the years, in the midst of the years make known; in wrath remember mercy.

God came from Teman, and the Holy One from mount Paran. Selah. His glory covered the heavens, and the earth was full of his praise. And his brightness was as the light; he had horns coming out of his hand: and there was the hiding of his power. Before him went the pestilence, and burning coals went forth at his feet. He stood, and measured the earth: he beheld, and drove asunder the nations; and the everlasting mountains were scattered, the perpetual hills did bow: his ways are everlasting. I saw the tents of Cushan in affliction: and the curtains of the land of Midian did tremble. Was the LORD displeased against the rivers? was your anger against the rivers? was your wrath against the sea, that you did ride upon your horses and

*your chariots of salvation? Your bow was made
quite naked, according to the oaths of the tribes,
even your word. Selah. You did cleave the earth
with rivers. The mountains saw you, and they trembled: the overflowing of the water passed by: the
deep uttered his voice and lifted up his hands on
high. The sun and moon stood still in their habitation: at the light of your arrows they went, and
at the shining of your glittering spear. You did
march through the land in indignation, you did
thresh the heathen in anger. You went forth for the
salvation of your people, even for salvation with
your anointed; you wounded the head out of the
house of the wicked, by discovering the foundation unto the neck. Selah. You did strike through
with his staves the head of his villages: they came
out as a whirlwind to scatter me: their rejoicing
was as to devour the poor secretly. You did walk
through the sea with your horses, through the heap
of great waters.*

*When I heard, my belly trembled; my lips quivered
at the voice: rottenness entered into my bones, and
I trembled in myself, that I might rest in the day
of trouble: when he comes up unto the people, he
will invade them with his troops. Although the fig
tree shall not blossom, neither shall fruit be in the
vines; the labor of the olive shall fail, and the fields
shall yield no meat; the flock shall be cut off from
the fold, and there shall be no herd in the stalls: Yet
I will rejoice in the LORD, I will joy in the God of
my salvation. The LORD God is my strength, and*

he will make my feet like hinds' feet, and he will
make me to walk upon mine high places. "To the
chief singer on my stringed instruments

T he third chapter of Habakkuk is titled *A Prayer of Habakkuk*
   the Prophet upon Shigionoth. The simple title indicates it
is a prayer of praise. The heading is similar to that of several
psalms, in which the contents, the author, and the character of
the song are indicated (e.g., Psalms 16, 30, 45, 88, 102, and 142).
Habakkuk again identifies himself as a prophet, as he had done at
the beginning of his book (1:1). Old Testament scholars identify
Habakkuk as a *minor prophet.* He ought rather to be classified as
a *major pray-er.*

A brief review is in order for us to see what is happening to the
Praying Prophet. Your attention is directed to chapter 3, verse 1.
There is a difference in the words used in 1:1 and the words chosen
for 3:1. But that change is so very heavy loaded with the freight
of what is being told us. In 1:1 we read:

The burden which Habakkuk the prophet did see.

Please observe the writer says *the burden.* He uses the definite
article. This use calls us to focus on a specific *burden* which God
gave to Habakkuk. The conversation recorded in by Habakkuk
will give a detailed account of that specific *burden* and how, with
God's direction, Habakkuk navigated through a very stormy period
of life. Also 1:1 directs our attention to the fact that Habakkuk *did*
see the *burden.* The words *did see* do not carry the idea of physical sight. They are a metaphorical use of the idea of mental sight,
or *insight.* They mean that Habakkuk came to understand clearly
the message which became a *burden* to him.

In 3:1, we see these words:

A prayer of Habakkuk the prophet upon Shigionoth.

Notice the article used here is an *A*. This indicates that no specific prayer is being set forth. What is given instead is an example, or a sample, of Habakkuk's praying.

The word *Shigionoth* of 3:1 is used only two times in the Old Testament. The other usage is found in the heading for Psalm 7. There is much discussion as to its actual meaning. Charles Spurgeon authored one of the most inclusive and thorough commentaries on the Psalms. It is known as *The Treasury of David*. Here are his comments about the word *Shigionoth* (שִׁגָּיוֹן) as found in Psalm 7:

> *As far as we can gather from the observations of learned men, and from a comparison of this Psalm with the only other Shiggaion in the Word of God (Habakkuk 3), this title seems to mean "variable songs," with which also the idea of solace and pleasure is associated.*

The word neginoth used in 3:19 seems to correspond favorably with *Shigionoth* of 3:1. Spurgeon's comments about that word are as follows:

> *On Neginoth, that is, on stringed instruments, or* hand *instruments, which were played on with the hand alone, as harps and cymbals. The joy of the Jewish church was so great that they needed music to set forth the delightful feelings of their souls, our*

holy mirth is none the less overflowing because we prefer to express it in a more spiritual manner, as becometh a more spiritual dispensation.

Chapter 1 discusses Habakkuk's problem. Habakkuk, the statesman/prophet, became deeply burdened by the rampant sin in the personal, political, public, and spiritual lives of his fellow citizens in Judah. The burden moved him to pray. This is what I have designated as *proxy praying* (praying for a person(s) who either cannot or will not pray for themselves.) on behalf of Judah. Apparently, he prayed earnestly and extensively about the matter. He complained in 1:2 – 4 that God was not listening to, or answering, his prayers. He cried out to God about the sin and violence of his day only to witness an violence increase (1:2-4).

God interrupted his complaining in 1:5:

Behold ye among the heathen, and regard, and wonder marvelously: For I will work a work in your days, Which ye will not believe, though it be told you.

God is telling the prophet to observe and study the *heathen* nations. He insisted that Habakkuk *regard* (inspect or spy out) the Gentile nations. In doing so Habakkuk would discover God doing an unbelievable work which would cause the prophet to *wonder marvelously.*

In 1:6-11 God reveals to Habakkuk that he is using the Chaldeans (Babylon) as his instrument to judge Judah. This was, in Habakkuk's mind, God acting in absolute contradiction to his character. Habakkuk's concept of God's character is found in

1:12-17. He uncovers his thinking that God actions are inconsistent with his character. But nonetheless he knows he is wrong, and that God will *reprove* him. He was shocked and amazed when God revealed to him that He had already prepared an instrument to use in judging Judah, namely Babylon. Habakkuk could not conceive of the idea that God would use a nation more sinful than Judah as His instrument of judgment.

Chapter 2:1 Habakkuk describes the course of action he has decided to follow:

> *I will stand upon my watch, and set me upon the*
> *tower, And will watch to see what he will say unto*
> *me, And what I shall answer when I am reproved.*

The action described here is stated in the form of a metaphor. This will be understood as you look at the words *stand* and *tower*, as well as the phrase *watch to see*. The words are not meant to describe the action of climbing up a watchtower. They rather picture Habakkuk's *attitude* and not his *altitude*. The prophet was learning that a person could see more when on their knees than could be seen from atop a watchtower. Elevation sometimes shrouds a person in a spiritual smog that prevents their have a clear vision of what God is doing.

I served as pastor in the Houston, Texas area for several years. Sometimes in the early morning as I would begin a drive into the downtown area on my way to the Medical Center, I would look ahead and discover an umbrella of smog hanging as a shroud over the area. As I drove on toward the city, I would think about how the vision of the residents was impaired by the smog cloud.

So, Habakkuk resolved to take a position from which he could *watch to see what he (God) will say to me.* There is the second clue that we are reading a metaphorical statement. Habakkuk was saying that he would *see* what God was *saying.* That statement has to be considered an oxymoron. We do not *see voices.* By use of the metaphor Habakkuk was declaring that he would understand clearly what God would say to him.

He knew that he would be *reproved* (תּוֹכֵחָה – *towkechah* [rebuke, or correct]) by God. The word *reprove* means *to be corrected.* He charged God with being derelict in his duty. God *corrected* him by persuading him to really observe and understand clearly what was being done. Habakkuk learned that God had, and was, in fact already answering his prayer. He was instructed to carefully and clearly record what he saw from the "watchtower." His record of God's answer took the form of a dirge, or taunting song (2:5-20). Learning of God's plan to destroy Babylon, Habakkuk bowed in humble adoration. His majestic prayer and hymn of praise followed.

Another fact worthy of note is that one of the reasons Habakkuk took a place on a tower was so that he would be able to "answer" God when He "reproved" him for his complaint. The answer he gave God is chapter 3 of his book.

In chapter 3 we see Habakkuk as a changed man! Instead of complaining, he is praising the Lord. God will also turn our sighing into singing if we (like Habakkuk) take time to watch and wait before Him in prayer and listen to His Word. As a result of this change, Habakkuk sings a prayer to God.

Chapter 3 begins with these words: *A prayer of Habakkuk the prophet upon Shigionoth. Shigionoth* literally means "to wander" or "to stray." Here it probably refers to a variety of song and music styles. In 3:19 the song is accompanied "on my stringed instruments." The word used for "stringed instruments" is *neginoth*, which is kin to the word *Shigionoth*. The chapter closes with these directions: "To the chief singer on my stringed instruments." The prophet-turned-songwriter has written a prayer song to be sung in a variety of styles and to be accompanied with stringed instruments.

There is nothing quite like a song to touch the soul and heart very deeply. Emotions were running, and still do run, very deep when dealing with the matter of prayer. Habakkuk sings a prayer to God. The prayer/song describes what he had learned about prayer while watching and waiting on the "tower."

PRECEPT # 13
Lessons Habakkuk learned about prayer.

The prayer expresses a heartfelt reverence for God (3:2-5):

> *O LORD, I have heard your speech, and was afraid: O LORD, revive your work in the midst of the years, in the midst of the years make known; in wrath remember mercy." God came from Teman and the Holy One from mount Paran. Selah. His glory covered the heavens, and the earth was full of his praise. And his brightness was as the light; he had horns coming out of his hand: and there was the hiding of his power. Before him went the pestilence, and burning coals went forth at his feet.*

In verse 3 Habakkuk recounts that he saw God coming from Teman and Mount Paran. This may be a reference to the appearances of God on Mt. Sinai. But the idea is that of God's approach toward Judah in judgment and toward Babylon in destruction. It was the Holy One (*qadosh* -קָדוֹשׁ) whom Habakkuk saw.

In verse 4 Habakkuk gives a description of the Holy One:

His radiance is like the sunlight; He has rays flashing from His hand, and there is the hiding of His power.

These words speak of the transcendence of God. The Apostle Paul saw him when on his way to Damascus as a light brighter than the noonday sun. Habakkuk's words are probably a reference to the Shekinah glory of God that stood between the people of Israel and the Egyptian army on the night of their deliverance. That cloud appeared to shelter them from the Egyptians so that they could cross the Red Sea. Later, it was God's radiant Shekinah glory that led them through their years of wandering in the desert.

The song of praise and prayer also contains a humble cry for revival from God (3:2):

O LORD, I have heard your speech, and was afraid: O LORD, revive your work in the midst of the years, in the midst of the years make known; in wrath remember mercy.

Habakkuk had heard God speak of his purposes to discipline Judah and destroy Babylon (1:5-11 and 2:3-20). The phrase "I have heard your speech," literally translated, would read, "I have heard the hearing of you." It is really an ancient but emphatic form of our contemporary expression "İ hear you," which means, "I hear, understand, and know what you mean by what you are saying."

My late wife and I were on a tour of London, England, with some friends. It was February, and the weather was extremely cold. We were up early to do some sightseeing and were standing near the Thames River waiting for the tour boat to take us to our destination. We decided that a cup of hot coffee would be good while we waited. I walked up to an Englishman standing nearby and asked if he knew where I could find some coffee. He spoke with a very pronounced English accent, and I did not understand his answer. I replied: "Pardon me, I did not hear what you said." To which he responded: "You heard me; you just did not understand." I learned then the distinction between hearing and understanding.

Habakkuk had probably heard God before he began writing his book. But he had not understood God. Now he understands God, and the distinction has filled him with awe. God's plans were beyond human understanding and God's preeminence beyond comprehension. The reaction to what he "heard" was to fear God. When this word *afraid* (יָרֵא -*yare*) is used for a person in an exalted position, it connotes "standing in awe." This is not simple fear but reverence and awe, whereby an individual recognizes the power and position of the individual revered and renders him proper respect.

In this song of praise and prayer, Habakkuk initially made two requests of God. He prayed for a fresh manifestation of God's power, "revive your work", and for an extension of "mercy." These were the only two petitions in his entire prayer.

The first request for renewal or revival of God's intervention was twice linked to time: "in the midst of the years" on both occasions. If paraphrased, the dual use of the expression would read "in our day and in our time." It seems that the prophet desired a prompt fulfillment. God had, of course, already promised such (1:5).

The word *revive* as used here, does not mean "revival" in the sense that it usually refers to a "revival meeting" in one of our churches. The contemporary church/Christian use of the word *revival* means "to bring to a new, fresh, or refreshed state of being." It means "to reanimate." Habakkuk has both heard and seen God at work bringing about justice and judgment. The experience produced in him a profound sense of reverence and brought him to a level of spiritual education that prompted him to ask for more. The use of the word revive (חָיָה–*chayah*) is a request for God to "make alive" or to "keep alive" his work (פֹּעַל–*po'al*). The word does not imply that there has been a lull or decline or a cessation of God's work. It rather expresses a strong desire for a work in progress to be kept alive.

The form of this word is interesting. It is in an intensive form and is in the imperative mood. Such a linguistic pattern as this shows a burdened, intensive, earnest request for God to take, or to continue, redemptive activity. Is this a prayer for God to resume what He had once done but is not now doing? Or is this a prayer for God to keep alive that which He has been doing all along? Habakkuk chapters 1 and 2 have already shown us what God has been, and is, doing. From his position on a "tower," Habakkuk has seen God doing "astonishing" things. He is here asking God to keep on doing what He is and has been doing. Habakkuk has learned that God is at work among the nations of His world, contrary to the perception voiced in his first complaint, that God was not doing anything in response to his prayer. Here in 3:3 he is not asking for the resumption or for a reanimation or for a reviving-to bring to life again-of God's work. He is asking that God keep alive His amazing activity.

Psalm 85 is a plea to God to revive his work:

> *LORD, thou hast been favorable unto thy land: thou hast brought back the captivity of Jacob. Thou hast forgiven the iniquity of thy people, thou hast covered all their sin. Selah. Thou hast taken away all thy wrath: thou hast turned thyself from the fierceness of thine anger. Turn us, O God of our salvation, and cause thine anger toward us to cease. Wilt thou be angry with us forever? wilt thou draw out thine anger to all generations? Wilt thou not revive us again: that thy people may rejoice in thee? Shew us thy mercy, O LORD, and grant us thy salvation.*

> *I will hear what God the LORD will speak: for he will speak peace unto his people, and to his saints: but let them not turn again to folly. Surely his salvation is nigh them that fear him; that glory may dwell in our land. Mercy and truth are met together; righteousness and peace have kissed each other. Truth shall spring out of the earth; and righteousness shall look down from heaven. Yea, the LORD shall give that which is good; and our land shall yield her increase. Righteousness shall go before him; and shall set us in the way of his steps.*

The prophet's second request evolved from the first. In these acts of judgment (wrath; cf. 3:8, 12) Habakkuk pleaded for mercy. He makes a request for God to show mercy along with his work of judgment. The word *mercy* (*racham-* רָחַם) means "to have compassion, to be merciful, pity." The verb is translated "love" once: "I will love you, O Lord" (Psalm 18:1).

God uses this word in promising to declare His name to Moses:

I will make all my goodness pass before you, and I will proclaim the name of the Lord before you; and will be gracious to whom I will be gracious and will show mercy on whom I will show mercy (Exodus 33:19).

The Psalm writer prayed:

Remember, O Lord, your tender mercies and your loving-kindnesses (Psalm 25:6).

And Isaiah prophesies messianic restoration, saying:

With great mercies will I gather you. But with everlasting kindness will I have mercy on you, says the Lord your Redeemer (Isaiah 54:7-8).

The concept carried by this word reveals the very heart of God's salvation.

Some years ago, I was made aware of the significance of "mercy" in connection with our sins. I was preaching for a "revival meeting" in a small rural community in East Texas. I had been impressed with what I thought was excessive pride on the part of one of the farmers in that community and church. That was a definite sin on my part to have a judgmental attitude toward the person. During the meeting, early in the week, the pastor asked that person to lead the congregation in prayer. At the close of his prayer, he made a statement that the Holy Spirit planted in my heart and has kept it alive since that evening many years ago. The statement was: "Lord, deal mercifully with us in our sin." That is not really such an unusual statement, but the Holy Spirit used it to convict me of a sinful act and attitude. When I read the statement of Habakkuk "in wrath remember mercy." I am again reminded of the need on our part for God's wrath to be tempered by and with His mercy. The "mercy seat" on the Ark of the Covenant in the Tabernacle serves to remind us of the need for a divinely provided covering for the law and its death penalties. That is what the "mercy seat" did. That is what Habakkuk is praying for.

Habakkuk's song of praise and prayer reveals a holy remembrance of God (3:6-16):

> *He stood, and measured the earth: he beheld, and drove asunder the nations; and the everlasting mountains were scattered, the perpetual hills did bow: his ways are everlasting. I saw the tents of Cushan in affliction: and the curtains of the land of Midian did tremble. Was the LORD displeased against the rivers? was your anger against the rivers? was your wrath against the sea, that you did ride upon your horses and your chariots of salvation? Your bow was made quite naked, according to the oaths of the tribes, even your word. Selah. You did cleave the earth with rivers. The mountains*

*saw you, and they trembled: the overflowing of the
water passed by: the deep uttered his voice, and
lifted up his hands on high. The sun and moon
stood still in their habitation: at the light of your
arrows they went, and at the shining of your glittering spear. You did march through the land in
indignation, you did thresh the heathen in anger.
You went forth for the salvation of your people, even
for salvation with your anointed; you wounded the
head out of the house of the wicked, by discovering
the foundation unto the neck. Selah. You did strike
through with his staves the head of his villages:
they came out as a whirlwind to scatter me: their
rejoicing was as to devour the poor secretly. You
did walk through the sea with your horses, through
the heap of great waters.*

*When I heard, my belly trembled; my lips quivered
at the voice: rottenness entered into my bones, and
I trembled in myself, that I might rest in the day of
trouble: when he comes up unto the people, he will
invade them with his troops.*

Selah (celah -סֶלָה) "to lift up, exalt": a technical musical term
probably showing accentuation, pause, interruption.

God's people, when in distress, feeling trapped in deep despair,
and facing what seemed certain defeat, looked at the "old days,"
the ancient times, when God went forth in victory for His people.
In their search for help, they, in their prayers, pleaded those days
and God's delivering work as a request for God to act in a similar
way on their behalf. In effect they were saying: "Do it again, Lord."

In 3:3-16 Habakkuk gives a list of what some say are the awesome deeds of God as He brought His people out of Egypt and led them through the wilderness into the Promised Land. The purpose of such a recitation of historical events is to express the prophet's confidence that God could also deliver His people from Babylon.

Habakkuk reviews the history of God's people and recounts some of the "astonishing" things God has done. It is possible that each of the activities attributed to God in this section of Habakkuk has reference to a specific event in the history of the nation(s). This cannot be said with dogmatism, but it is well within the realm of possibility. For example, read 3:3-4:

> *God came from Teman, and the Holy One from mount Paran. Selah. His glory covered the heavens, and the earth was full of his praise. And his brightness was as the light; he had horns coming out of his hand: and there was the hiding of his power.*

The "cloudy pillar" of Exodus 13:20-22 may be in mind here:

> *And they took their journey from Succoth, and encamped in Etham, in the edge of the wilderness. And the LORD went before them by day in a pillar of a cloud, to lead them the way; and by night in a pillar of fire, to give them light; to go by day and night: He took not away the pillar of the cloud by day, nor the pillar of fire by night, from before the people.*

Habakkuk 3:5-6 reveals some additional lessons the prophet learned about prayer:

Before him went the pestilence, and burning coals went forth at his feet. He stood, and measured the earth: he beheld, and drove asunder the nations; and the everlasting mountains were scattered, the perpetual hills did bow: his ways are everlasting.

In 3:7-8 Habakkuk may have a reference to the plagues God brought upon Egypt:

I saw the tents of Cushan in affliction: and the curtains of the land of Midian did tremble. Was the LORD displeased against the rivers? was your anger against the rivers? was your wrath against the sea, that you did ride upon your horses and your chariots of salvation? Your bow was made quite naked, according to the oaths of the tribes, even your word. Selah. You did cleave the earth with rivers.

This seems to speak of events such as those of Deuteronomy 2:24-25:

Rise you up, take your journey, and pass over the river Arnon: behold, I have given into your hand Sihon the Amorite, king of Heshbon, and his land: begin to possess it, and contend with him in battle. This day will I begin to put the dread of you and the fear of you upon the nations that are under the whole heaven, who shall hear report of you, and shall tremble, and be in anguish because of you.

We also read in Habakkuk 3:10:

The mountains saw you, and they trembled: the overflowing of the water passed by; the deep uttered his voice and lifted up his hands on high.

This could be speaking about Mt. Sinai and Exodus 19:16:

And it came to pass on the third day in the morning, that there were thunders and lightnings, and a thick cloud upon the mount, and the voice of the trumpet exceeding loud; so that all the people that was in the camp trembled.

The statement made in 3:11 could possibly have reference to the event described in Joshua:

The sun and moon stood still in their habitation: at the light of your arrows they went, and at the shining of your glittering spear.

Perhaps it refers to Joshua 10:12-13:

Then spoke Joshua to the LORD in the day when the LORD delivered up the Amorites before the children of Israel, and he said in the sight of Israel, Sun, you stand still upon Gibeon; and you, Moon, in the valley of Ajalon. And the sun stood still, and the moon stayed, until the people had avenged themselves upon their enemies. Is not this written in the book of Jasher? So, the sun stood still in

*the midst of heaven, and hastened not to go down
about a whole day.*

Habakkuk 3:12 seems to be speaking about the years of the wilderness wandering of Israel:

*You did march through the land in indignation, you
did thresh the heathen in anger* (v. 12).

Chapter 3:15 is obviously referring the event of Exodus 15:8:

*You did walk through the sea with your horses,
through the heap of great waters.*

*And with the blast of your nostrils the waters were
gathered together, the floods stood upright as an
heap, and the depths were congealed in the heart
of the sea.*

The idea conveyed by the metaphor of horses and water may paint a picture of there being no insurmountable barriers to God. There are no mountains God cannot scale, no rivers God cannot ford, and no valleys God cannot cross.

It seems a bit strange, but this trail of cross-referencing Scripture leads us to a possible explanation of God parting the waters of the sea to allow Israel to cross it as they made their exodus from Egypt. Some translations of the verse of Exodus 15:8 use the word *congealed* (קָפָא—*qapha*). The word (עָרַם -ʿ*aram*) is translated in the KJV as "gathered together." The word *congealed* paints a picture in clear, vivid colors and broad strokes of a body of water being divided into two parts, with each part forming a "congealed" body of water. This constitutes a very enlightening description of the mighty power of God to deliver. Habakkuk could not have chosen a clearer picture of God's mighty power to deliver his people. Habakkuk's prayer could have no more definite and positive answer.

In the first section of this study of the conversation between God and Habakkuk about prayer and the answer- or the assumed failure of God to answer–I introduced two possible forms of praying. At this point a return to our study of those two forms of praying– *circumstance oriented* prayer and/or *fellowship oriented* prayer -is in order. Also, at this junction application of that concept is easily made.

The reader will observe the use of the word *oriented*. The word places the focus of a prayer. The word also points to the motive for the prayer. The circumstances out of which a prayer is birthed give the prayer its direction and provide the controlling factors that determine its effectiveness. Attention is redirected to the passages in Colossians 4:2 and 1 Thessalonians 5:17. Colossians 4:2 reads:

> *Continue in prayer and watch in the same with thanksgiving.*

And 1 Thessalonians 5:17 says:

> *Pray without ceasing.*

In the early reference, attention was directed to the words *continue* and *without ceasing*. Taken together these words present a style of praying that is frequent and repetitive. As such the prayer becomes the basis of an unbroken fellowship with God that assumes the form of a *dialogue*.

The 1 Thessalonians verse has the Greek word for "without ceasing" (one word in the Greek), which means to pray frequently and spontaneously. Fellowship oriented prayer means that the Believer prays frequently and spontaneously and has fellowship with Jesus Christ in a regular and unremitting pattern. It seems that *circumstance oriented* prayer will take the form of a monologue in which the Believer is the principle, if not the only, speaker. On the other hand, *fellowship oriented* prayer will assume the form of a dialogue with both God and the Believer participating in the conversation. In this form the prayer originates in an event that is rather normal and does not appear to be a crisis. *Fellowship oriented* prayer allows the Believer and God to converse with each other about a matter that does not command such a dominant influence upon the conversation. This means that fellowship is possible even while discussing any issue regardless of the gravity of the issue.

In chapter 2 of Habakkuk, he took refuge upon (within) a "watchtower," from which he was to discover what God would say in correcting or rebuking him. Habakkuk's understanding and practice of prayer had been proven to be in error. Because of this, he assumed God was neither listening nor answering his prayer. The outgrowth from this misunderstanding and practice resulted in his indictment of God for failing to answer his prayer.

Chapter 3 of Habakkuk is a prayer. It is a musical prayer. He gives the instructions that it be sung with a variety of accompanying instrumentation. The chapter is really a praise prayer detailing his experience with God in the school of prayer. He helps his readers gain a better understanding of prayer (*fellowship oriented* prayer) by reviewing some of the work of God. Habakkuk provides validation by means of a catalog of events recorded previously in the Old Testament.

A review of the characteristics of *fellowship oriented* prayer is in order. The 1 Thessalonians verse has the word for "without ceasing," which means to pray frequently and spontaneously. As previously noted, this form of prayer becomes a *dialogue*. Both God and the Believer are involved in the conversation. Whereas *circumstance oriented* prayer finds the Believer to be the featured, if not the only, speaker, and the prayer becomes only a *monologue*. In this form the Believer determines the conditions under which the prayer takes place. The subject, the importance of the subject, the urgency of the issue discussed, the form and time of the answer, etc. are all stated. It is easy to see that this prayer is *circumstance oriented*.

The negative aspect of *circumstance oriented* prayer is discovered in its focus upon the circumstances in which the Believer is found.

1. That focus deprives the Believer of a clear grasp of God's character. (1:12-13).

2. It makes the prevailing circumstance the dominant factor in the prayer and often obscures the awareness of God (1:3-4).

3. It encourages the Believer to indict God as not listening and responding to the prayer (1:2).

4. It prevents the Believer from seeing and recognizing God's answer (1:5-6).

5. It becomes a handicap to the Believer's developing a Biblical worldviewof God's plans and activity (1:12-17).

This list could be greatly extended. However, these negative aspects are enough to help us see the nature of this form of prayer. These and other aspects help us in our evaluation of the form of prayer followed by Habakkuk at the beginning of the conversation. It was the form I am designating as *circumstance oriented* that caused Habakkuk to seek refuge in a watchtower. He had come to realize that he was incorrectly and improperly indicting God as not listening to and answering his prayer. He came to understand that the misunderstood and inaccurately described action of God had put him in jeopardy of God's rebuke and correction. For these reasons, he sought a refuge in which he could entertain God's rebuke. Chapter 2 describes to us his encounter and conversation with God while on (or in) the watchtower. It is in this period of time described in chapter 2 that Habakkuk details the lessons about prayer in which God instructs him.

In Habakkuk chapter 3, the prophet is presented to us as a corrected and converted person of prayer. He is shown in this chapter to have no remaining vestiges of doubt about God's answer to his prayer. To him there is no such experience as unanswered prayer. When prayer is a matter of fellowship with God and takes place within the skeleton of a dialogue, the answer can be easily detected when it comes. In such an atmosphere, faith in God's dependability to respond to our prayer can be maintained and developed. And God's character can be discovered, and His fellowship can be enjoyed. The lessons on prayer taught to him in chapter 2 are employed as he writes his own praise prayer recorded in chapter 3. That prayer is analyzed in the previous discussion found earlier in this section of our study.

PRECEPT # 14
Answered prayer prompts complete commitment.

Although the fig tree shall not blossom, neither shall fruit be in the vines; the labor of the olive shall fail, and the fields shall yield no meat; the flock shall be cut off from the fold, and there shall be no herd in the stalls: Yet I will rejoice in the LORD, I will joy in the God of my salvation. (Habakkuk 3:17-18)

In this passage Habakkuk may have reference to the days of Elijah. The point being made is that God told Habakkuk that if he would carefully observe contemporary history, he would "regard and wonder marvelously" (1:5). Now after his time spent on the watchtower, Habakkuk is keenly aware of the awesome things God has (and is) doing in his world.

Also found in the prayer/song is a healthy recommitment to God:

Although the fig tree shall not blossom, neither shall fruit be in the vines; the labor of the olive shall fail, and the fields shall yield no meat; the flock shall be cut off from the fold, and there shall be no herd in the stalls: Yet I will rejoice in the LORD, I will joy in the God of my salvation. The LORD God is my strength, and he will make my feet like hinds' feet, and he will make me to walk upon mine high places. (Habakkuk 3:17-19

These verses contain one of the great confessions of faith found in the Bible. Habakkuk now knows that God has and does hear and answer prayer. He also knows that judgment is coming. The

176

absence of fruit and flock may be a somewhat veiled reference to the possible means of judgment available to God. He resolves and commits to God that whatever God does, he will be faithful.

> *Although the fig tree shall not blossom, neither shall fruit be in the vines; the labor of the olive shall fail, and the fields shall yield no meat; the flock shall be cut off from the fold, and there shall be no herd in the stalls: Yet I will rejoice in the LORD, I will joy in the God of my salvation.*

The climactic statement and/or confession made by the prophet Habakkuk is found in 3:19:

> *LORD God is my strength, and he will make my feet like hinds' feet, and he will make me to walk upon mine high places.*

The significance and magnitude of these words are attested to by the fact that they are found in two other places in the Bible.

First, 2 Samuel 22:1, 33, 34, which predate Habakkuk, attribute the words to David as his testimony of praise to God when he delivered him from Saul. David sang this song:

> *And David spoke unto the LORD the words of this song in the day that the LORD had delivered him out of the hand of all his enemies, and out of the hand of Saul:... God is my strength and power: and he makes my way perfect. He makes my feet like hinds' feet: and sets me upon my high places.*

Psalm 18 is apparently a quotation of the 2 Samuel passage. Psalm 18:1, 33, read:

> *To the chief Musician, A Psalm of David, the servant of the LORD, who spoke unto the LORD the words of this song in the day that the LORD delivered him from the hand of all his enemies, and from the hand of Saul: And he said, I will love thee, O LORD, my strength... For who is God, save the LORD? and who is a rock, save our God? God is my strength and power: and he makes my way perfect. He makes my feet like hinds' feet: and sets me upon my high places.*

It therefore seems highly possible that Habakkuk is quoting David and using David's words to express his testimony and praise to God. It is the testimony of one who has found "strength" (חַיִל–*chayil*) in *Jehovah Adonai* (יְהוָה אֲדֹנָי),[4] his *LORD God,* or his *LORD and God.* The word for *strength* is based upon a word that means "to dance" or "to whirl about." It would seem that Habakkuk has reference to the joy that resulted from what he has seen and learned about God answering prayer. When he quotes David's metaphor of the deer's feet, he is speaking not so much about the ability to climb to high places as about agility to negotiate the complex issues of life. The metaphor seems to reference *attitude* and not *altitude*. It is not so much speaking about *physical elevation* as about *spiritual elation*. The wording of these verses in 2 Samuel 22, Psalm 18, and Habakkuk 3 connotes light-heartedness and the graceful movement of exhilarated and reverent dancing before God. The writers, David and Habakkuk, are experiencing and expressing

---

[4] Further study of this name of God can be found in my book *His Excellent Name,* p. 190; copyright Xulon Press 2009.

a deep awe and reverence for God. The whole of Habakkuk 3 is in the form of a song of praise—exhilarating music sung to the God who has indeed heard and answered his prayer for Judah, his people, and his nation.

A Synopsis

T he main truth to be learned about prayer is that the main objective of prayer is to glorify God. It is not to supply some personal need of an individual. As we glorify God, our needs are supplied. The need is supplied in the process of glorifying God. Personal needs are secondary to the glory of God.

And call upon me in the day of trouble: I will deliver you, and you shall glorify me. (Ps. 50:15)

Chapter digest:

1. ASK—then TRUST (Habakkuk 1)
2. ASK—then WATCH (Habakkuk 2)
3. ASK—then PRAISE (Habakkuk 3)

VERSES FOR MEDITATION:

Habakkuk 1:13 -"Your eyes are too pure to approve evil, And You can not look on wickedness with favor."

Habakkuk 2:4 -"Behold, his soul which is lifted up is not upright in him: but the just shall live by his faith."

Habakkuk 2:14 -"For the earth shall be filled with the knowledge of the glory of the LORD, as the waters cover the sea."

Habakkuk 2:20 -"But the LORD is in his holy temple: let all the earth keep silence before him."

Habakkuk 3:17-18 -"Although the fig tree shall not blossom, neither shall fruit be in the vines; the labor of the olive shall fail, and the fields shall yield no meat; the flock shall be cut off from the fold, and there shall be no herd in the stalls: Yet I will rejoice in the LORD, I will joy in the God of my salvation."

Habakkuk 3:19 -"The LORD God is my strength, and he will make my feet like hinds' feet, and he will make me to walk upon mine high places."

Babel Revisited

This addendum is added to focus the teachings of Habakkuk on a topic that in some ways, at least, is one of the hottest of contemporary subjects. The church must come to a biblical worldview of this subject. The subject to which I refer is that of immigration. The contemporary patterns of immigration have a striking similarity to the population and language pattern chronicled in Genesis 11. And in Habakkuk is found a strong urge for Believers to develop a Biblical worldview. The ascendency of Babylon (the Chaldeans of Habakkuk) seems to paint a picture of a rather cosmopolitan world. The influence of Babylonian culture had spread and permeated most every nation of that world. Our contemporary world is little different. Therefore, I present these thoughts for consideration as the church seeks to evangelize its world.

And the LORD came down to see the city and the tower, which the children of men builded. And the LORD said, Behold, the people is one, and they have all one language; and this they begin to do: and now nothing will be restrained from them, which they have imagined to do. Go to, let us go down, and there confound their language, that they may not understand one another's speech. So, the LORD scattered them abroad from thence upon the face of all the earth: and they left off to build the city. Therefore,

> *is the name of it called Babel; because the* LORD *did*
> *there confound the language of all the earth: and*
> *from thence did the* LORD *scatter them abroad upon*
> *the face of all the earth.* (Genesis 11:5-9)

The operative statements in this passage are "the people is one," "they have all one language," and "nothing will be restrained from them." The word *Babel* (בָּבֶל–*Babel*) is thought by many commentators to derive from *balal* (בָּלַל–baw·lal), which means "mingled," "confusion," and "mixed." Their congregating geographically contributed to their consolidating linguistically, which resulted in their ability to do anything they "imagined."

When Habakkuk finishes his prayer and then describes Babylon and her influence upon him, we get the idea that he still does not understand God's plan for Israel being captured and deported to Babylon. It appears throughout history that God's people seem never really to understand what God is doing through other nations. The salvation of the unbelieving population of the world is always of primary importance to God.

While the Jews were in Egypt, they never understood why God put them there. In the days of Moses, God told the ruler of Egypt that he had been placed in power in order that he might be used to glorify God (Exodus 9:16). But the Jews never understood this. They merely complained and cried out to God because of their hardship. Those who went to Egypt with Jacob spent 430 years in that place as servants, or maybe better described as slaves. All the while they never seemed to realize that God was at work in Egypt in ways that would bring glory to His name.

Now God reveals to Habakkuk his plans to allow Judah to be conquered and deported to Babylon. He has revealed to Jeremiah, and Daniel has understood Jeremiah's prophesy, that they would remain in Babylon for seventy years. But when they had arrived in Babylon, they became very discouraged and depressed. Their state of mind and spirit is described in Psalm 137:1-4:

> *By the rivers of Babylon, there we sat down, yes, we wept, when we remembered Zion. We hung our harps upon the willows in the midst thereof. For there they that carried us away captive required of us a song; and they that wasted us required of us mirth, saying, Sing us one of the songs of Zion. How shall we sing the LORD'S song in a strange land?*

The Psalm clearly indicates the great opportunity they had to give witness to the greatness of their God—a God unknown to Babylon. But their response was to ask:

> *"How shall we sing the LORD'S song in a strange land?"*

The real question is, "How could they *not* sing the Lord's song while in Babylon?" What better place could they find to sing? What better remedy could be found for their depression than singing the Lord's song? What better means could they find to witness to a godless nation? Read Isaiah 48:20 in this context:

> *Go you forth of Babylon, flee you from the Chaldeans, with a voice of singing declare you, tell this, utter it even to the end of the earth; say you, The LORD has redeemed his servant Jacob."*

Some who were deported to Babylon did indeed give a strong and effective witness for God. In Daniel 1:6 four persons are named -Daniel, Hananiah, Mishael, and Azariah. The name of Daniel we recognize, but the other three we may not remember. They were renamed by Melzar, the prince of the eunuchs in Babylon. The names given them were Shadrach, Meshack, and Abednego. Daniel made a firm commitment that he would not become defiled by the diet and drink offered by the king. He became the interpreter of dreams for the rulers in Babylon. God used him to communicate his message and plans to those leaders of Babylon.

Nebuchadnezzar, ruler of Babylon, in his pride, made a gold image and ordered everyone to fall before it and worship. The three just mentioned whose names were changed refused to bow. We know the story well of how they were thrown into a furnace of fire. The story is recounted in Daniel 3. When Nebuchadnezzar came to check on the three, he discovered that God had protected and saved them from the fire. He acknowledged that God had done so (Daniel 3:28). Furthermore, he ordered that no one speak against the God of the three.

In Daniel 4 we have recorded the story of Nebuchadnezzar's pride. Because of his pride God allowed him to become rather insane and to live with the wild animals out in nature. He became like the animals in both looks and nature until he came to himself and realized what God was doing. The story of his recovery is given in Daniel 4:34:

> *And at the end of the days I Nebuchadnezzar lifted*
> *up my eyes unto heaven, and my understanding*
> *returned unto me, and I blessed the Most High,*
> *and I praised and honored him that lives forever,*

whose dominion is an everlasting dominion, and his kingdom is from generation to generation:

In the story of these four persons, we see a clear and convincing witness given concerning the person, purposes, and work of God. The rest of Judah seemed to miss the opportunity.

Now this leads me to the application to be made to the twenty-first-century Christians and churches, particularly in the United States of America. Our nation is being overrun by the immigration of people from other nations. We are particularly troubled and concerned by the large number of immigrants flowing across our borders into our country. Great emphasis and attention is given to the crisis created by the responsibility to care for the teeming mass of people trying to enter America. God has allowed our nation to become financially wealthy and blessed us with abundant resources. The other ethnic groups of people see what God is doing for America and they desire to enjoy a similar standard of living.

God has benefited the United States with a basic Christian philosophy as the foundation of our society. Although the effects of that philosophy are diminishing rapidly, it has been a determining factor in the development of this nation. God has allowed us more than a century of time in which to share the gospel with other nations. Some effort has been effective in that endeavor, but that effect is also diminishing.

My questions are these: Could it be that we have failed to carry the gospel to them and therefore God is bringing them to us? Will we continue to do battle over how to deal with this phenomenon and fail to realize that we must by all means, and in every way possible present the gospel to them? Will we continue to argue about providing education for them and fail to discover how to bring them to conversion? Will we continue to be so engulfed in the task of providing healthcare and healing and fail to see that their "sin-sickness" is their worst disease?

Why is God allowing this phenomenon to happen? God spoke to Habakkuk in 1:5, saying:

> *Behold you among the heathen, and regard, and wonder marvelously: for I will work a work in your days, which you will not believe, though it be told you.*

Could it be that God is gathering this massive number of people (or allowing them to gather) with the plan for them to hear the gospel and as Habakkuk says in Chapter 2 verses 13 and 14:

> *Behold, is it not of the LORD of hosts that the people shall labor in the very fire, and the people shall weary themselves for very vanity? For the earth shall be filled with the knowledge of the glory of the LORD, as the waters cover the sea.*

Thus, Habakkuk's ultimate prayer is:

> *O LORD, I have heard thy speech, and was afraid: O LORD, revive thy work in the midst of the years, in the midst of the years make known; in wrath remember mercy.*

CPSIA information can be obtained
at www.ICGtesting.com
Printed in the USA
JSHW031950090221
11760JS00001B/25

9 781662 809309